skills for success

passing HIGHER HISTORY

Ian Matheson

skills for success

passing HIGHER HISTORY

Ian Matheson

Hodder & Stoughton

A MEMBER OF THE HODDER HEADLINE GROUP

Acknowledgements

The publishers would like to thank the following people for their permission to reproduce copyright material:
HarperCollins Publishers for *Europe of the Dictators 1919–45* by Elizabeth Wiskemann (p. 9); Scottish Examination
Board of History, Paper I Option C, 1992 (p. 18), Paper I Option C, 1993 (pp. 19, 20, 21), Paper I Option C, 1994
(p. 19); Wiedenfield & Nicolson *Industry and Empire* by Eric Hobsbawm (p. 43); Scottish Examination Board of
History *Revised Arrangements in History* (p. 45); *The Times* 1 October 1938 (p. 48); Longman for *Britain and Germany
between the Wars* by Martin Gilbert (pp. 50, 51); Simon & Schuster for *Contemporary Europe: A History* by H Stuart
Hughes (p. 62); Dryad Press for *The Easter Rising* by Nathaniel Harris (p. 64), Penguin for *The Gathering Storm* by
Winston Churchill (p. 73) and *The Age of Upheaval: The World Since 1914* by JM Roberts (p. 74) and *From Yalta to
Vietnam* by David Horowitz (p. 77).

The publishers would like to thank the following for their permission to reproduce copyright illustrations:
Cover: (clockwise from above) Topham Picture Point; Hulton Deutsch; Topham Picture Point; Hulton Deutsch;
Topham Picture Point; Topham Picture Point; Back cover: Hulton Deutsch; pages 56, 58, 78, Punch Publications;
page 74 David Low, *Evening Standard*, Centre for the Study of Cartoons and Caricature, University of Kent.

British Library Cataloguing in Publication Data
A catalogue for this title is available from the British Library

ISBN 0 340 65555 0

First published 1996
Impression number   10 9 8 7 6 5 4 3 2 1
Year   1999 1998 1997 1996

Typeset by Fakenham Photosetting Ltd, Fakenham, Norfolk
Printed in Great Britain for Hodder & Stoughton Educational, a division of Hodder Headline Plc, 338 Euston Road,
London NW1 3BH by The Bath Press

Contents

Introduction

The purpose of this book is to help candidates to learn the skills tested in Option C: Later Modern History of the Higher History examination. It deals with all three elements of the examination: preparing for the Extended Essay, essay writing technique and working with sources.

In offering advice on these skills I have tried to show that a logical approach can make them much simpler to master than they appear at first sight. I have included examples of potential tasks and questions, with suggestions on how these could be answered effectively. Most of these have been taken from the most popular areas of study, Sections (a) and (b) of the General Study and the Special Topic *Appeasement and the Road to War, to 1939*. Other areas of the syllabus have not been ignored, especially in the Tasks, for which suggested solutions are given. Examples have been included, in particular from *The Large Scale State: Russia* and from the Special Topics on Patterns of Migration, the Cold War and Ireland. I hope that these will be of practical help to those preparing to sit this examination.

Many sources in the examination have been edited to assist candidates. When I have used sources that have appeared in past papers I have used these edited versions to avoid confusion.

TO THE CANDIDATE

If you prepare properly, learning the skills as well as the factual knowledge needed to help you demonstrate them properly, you can face the examination with confidence.

Remember, the examiners are not trying to catch you out. They want to set questions that will allow you to show what you *can* do and what you *have* learned.

Good luck with your examination, though if you have done your preparation you should not really need it!

Ian Matheson

SECTION 1

The Extended Essay

BACKGROUND

At Standard Grade you began to learn the skills of historical enquiry by carrying out an Investigation into an issue. This involved selecting an issue, planning your approach, carrying out research and reporting your conclusions. It was also a valuable exercise because it allowed you to take responsibility for some of your own learning.

It is important that you continue to develop these skills during your Higher Grade course, but the shorter length of the course makes it impossible to carry out as large a task as your Investigation. This has led to the creation of the Extended Essay based on a limited piece of research on an issue which you choose yourself after discussion with your teacher. You are then given two hours in which to write it up under examination conditions.

PURPOSES

The Extended Essay has several purposes.

- To build upon the skills of investigating begun at Standard Grade.
- To help you to take more responsibility for your own learning.
- To help you to develop the skill of planning an essay.
- To give you the chance to study in more depth an aspect of the course which interests you.
- To let you show off your best work by writing an essay without the strict time limits of Paper I and without having to rely on your memory for all the information you need.

The last of these points is especially important. An Extended Essay is no different in style from an essay written in answer to a question in Paper I. Only the circumstances have changed – *in your favour*.

CHOOSING AN ISSUE

The rules of the examination place only one restriction on your choice of issue – it must come from the syllabus of the course you are studying. You may choose a title from topics you cover in Paper I or from the Special Topic you are taking for Paper II.

In practice, you would be wise to add a few restrictions of your own. A good issue for an Extended Essay should be one:

- which you are confident you understand. The task is challenging enough without picking an area of history you find too difficult.
- in which you have a special interest. This stands to reason. If you are really interested in a topic, you are much more likely to enjoy doing the extra work needed to research it in some depth.
- on which it is reasonably easy to obtain good evidence, from the History department or from the school or public library.
- which is phrased as a proper question. This allows you to write an essay using skills like the selection and analysis of evidence, evaluation of historical events, debate and drawing a conclusion.

Give Yourself a Focus

If you choose an issue which is phrased clearly, it can give you a good focus for your work. It helps your research, because you can use it to judge whether the information you find is worth noting. By asking the question, 'Does this help me to reach a conclusion about my issue?' you can avoid going off on side tracks and so save a great deal of valuable time.

A clearly phrased issue will also help when it comes to writing up your essay, because it will help you to select the most relevant evidence and to organise it in a sensible way, so providing a good structure for your argument.

 If you wanted to write an Extended Essay on the suffragette movement in Britain, which of these titles might best help you to focus your research and your writing?

1 Who was Emmeline Pankhurst and what did she do to help women to gain the vote?
2 The Women's Social and Political Union.
3 How important was the WSPU in helping women to gain the vote?
4 Was the suffragette movement a success?
5 What methods did suffragettes use in this campaign?

Now compare your opinion with my thoughts on these questions on pages 13–14.

Be Practical

When choosing your issue it is important to make sure you set yourself a fair task, avoiding issues that are too complex or demanding. The temptation to try to impress the examiners by writing on an unusual topic may be attractive. You may be fascinated by the Nazi propaganda campaign aimed at the farmers of

Schleswig and Holstein in 1929. But you are unlikely to be able to research such a specialised issue in the time available. Choose a more practicable theme. Don't commit yourself to one which will require more research time than you can really afford, especially as you may well have other examinations to prepare for as well as History. In any case, the examiners will be much more impressed by the quality of your work than by the obscurity or individuality of your issue.

Besides being over specialised, issues can be too demanding in other ways. Even one which appears to link directly to a major theme in the syllabus can ask too much, not in research, but in planning and writing the essay.

Suppose you want to write about the rise of the Nazis to power in Germany. Consider these three questions. Which might you cope with and which might present unreasonable demands?

1 Compare the importance of anger over Versailles, the weaknesses of the Weimar Republic, economic depression, political violence and propaganda in explaining the Nazi rise to power.
2 Discuss the view that the Nazi seizure of power in 1933 was due less to long-term factors than to short-term mistakes made by individuals.
3 Explain why the Nazis came to power in 1933 and why they were able to stay in power until World War II.

Now compare your opinions with mine on page 14. When writing your own issue, write down several ways in which it could be phrased and choose the one which is most likely to help you to prepare and write your essay to the best of your ability.

RESEARCHING YOUR ESSAY

Once you have identified your issue, your next task is to find enough information to allow you to analyse it and draw a conclusion about it.

It is valuable at this stage to prepare a rough plan by analysing the question, as though you were preparing an essay for the written paper (see Section 2, pp. 17–22). This will allow you to identify the various factors or themes involved in your main issue, which will then form the focus for your research. Suppose, for instance, you have chosen an issue from the Special Topic, *Appeasement and the Road to War, to 1939*, relating to the appeasement policy followed by Britain during the second half of the 1930s. Examine the issue below:

How justified was the British Government in following a policy of appeasement between 1936 and 1939?

The factors you could consider in tackling this question might include public opinion in Britain during the '30s, British politicians' attitudes towards Fascism and Communism, the economic depression, the state of the armed forces and the policies of potential allies such as France. These factors now become the main themes about which you are trying to find evidence – though it is as well to remember that you may not have thought of all the possible influences at the start. As you are researching, keep a look out for some other factor that could turn out to be important and affect your conclusions.

Sources

Your starting point in most cases will be your existing knowledge of the topic from your class work, together with any notes and textbooks which your teacher can provide. For the Extended Essay, though, you should be looking to use other sources as well. You may be able to trace suitable books or articles through your school or public library, but often the best place to look for ideas is in the bibliography in your textbook. This should indicate other books suitable for senior school students, as well as some of the more approachable works written by professional historians.

In choosing your sources it is important not to make unreasonable demands on yourself, by attempting to read too many specialised historical works which could be very long. You do, after all, only have a few weeks in which to carry out your research, and there will be other demands on your time. Nonetheless, it is still good practice to read some history at the highest level you can cope with, because in this way you will be introduced to historical debate.

Historians are always disagreeing – often quite violently. (It has been said that if you put ten historians together you will find eleven opinions!) The topic of appeasement, mentioned above, has nearly brought some historians to blows. This makes it important that you understand in what ways they disagree and why they do so. The best way for you to do this is by reading some of the things they have written, to see how different selections or interpretations of evidence can lead people to very different conclusions.

A good rule in judging how much of a serious history book you need to read for this purpose is to remember that a good book shares many of the qualities of a good essay. The author must set out the main issues in the introduction and summarise the argument in the conclusion. In many cases these sections, especially the conclusion, will be the most useful for you to read.

An alternative to reading full length books is to look for shorter articles. There are several popular historical magazines (at least one is aimed at senior school students) which contain lively articles on topics which may be relevant to your chosen issue. Some articles present a single author's view, while occasionally you may find one which summarises a debate by reviewing the works of several authors. These magazines may also include book reviews, which can be useful examples of debate in action.

Taking Notes

There is no single way of taking notes that works for everyone. You must find a style that suits you. At the same time, the system you use must *work*; it must help you to organise your information and allow you to find it when you need it.

Here is a system that works for me. Perhaps it can help you too. When considering the question on appeasement, I would identify these five possible factors:

- British public opinion in the 1930s
- The attitudes of British politicians towards Fascism and Communism
- The economic depression
- The fear of aerial bombing
- The policies of potential allies.

Each of these factors is given a page of its own. While researching, all the information that is found about that factor goes on the same page, with a note to say where it came from, a code to say whether it represents fact (F) or opinion (O) and one to say whether the source is primary (P) or Secondary (S). It could look something like this:

BRITISH PUBLIC OPINION IN THE 1930s Information	F/O	P/S
Public opinion would not support military action or even economic sanctions against Germany at the time of the reoccupation of the Rhineland. The British people saw Hitler's actions as less aggressive than Mussolini's in Abyssinia. At least he had not invaded another country. *Speech in Parliament by Hugh Dalton, a Labour MP, 20 March 1936.*	O	P
February 1933 – Oxford Union Society debate on the motion that 'This House will in no circumstances fight for its King and Country'. The motion was passed. Around this time meetings held by peace movements attracted large crowds. In October 1934 the Peace Pledge Union was founded; within a year 80 000 people had signed a promise not to fight in a war. *David Thomson,* England in the Twentieth Century, *Pelican, 1965, pp. 156–157.*	F	S

In this way, all the information related to this factor stays together, which helps in organising it later. The sheets themselves can be rearranged to help put the factors in the most effective order. This makes the original plan for the essay flexible. It can change to reflect your own changing opinions as your research progresses. Having a separate sheet – or more likely several sheets – for each theme also allows for the possibility that a new factor may emerge in the course of the research without confusing the notes. The new one can have a sheet of its own.

Another benefit of organising your material in this way is that it helps you to see at a glance how your work is progressing. It can be very helpful to carry out a quick review from time to time, and to discuss your progress with your teacher, who may notice something that you have missed. In this way, you can obtain good guidance for the next stage.

Looking back to the original five factors for the research on appeasement, part of the way through your research you may have, say, four pages of notes on British public opinion in the 1930s, two each on British politicians' attitudes towards Fascism and Communism and on the state of the armed forces, a few lines on the policies of potential allies and nothing at all on the economic depression or the fear of aerial bombing. This could suggest that you need to concentrate more on areas in which there is a shortage of information – or it could suggest that one or more of these factors is not really important at all, and ought to be dropped from the plan. You would only find out by looking specifically for these areas when you continue your research. Perhaps a new factor, say news of rearmament in Nazi Germany, has appeared in the early stages of your research, so you have given it a separate sheet and are now looking for more information on that as well.

Your Words or Their Words?

Often human beings are lazy. They like to do things using the least mental energy possible. While making notes, this shows itself in the temptation to copy out pieces of the source word for word. Try to resist this temptation, as it can lead to writing out large quantities of information without thinking about it. A much better practice is to *summarise* the information in your own words, picking out the points that are important to your issue. This way, you have to think about what the source actually means, so increasing your own understanding of the author's point of view and of the historical issue itself. Even the simple process of making notes, therefore, can contribute to your own learning process.

3

1   Copy out this passage, word for word.

Many British politicians were reluctant to believe that Hitler wanted war in the West; and they regarded war in the East as a potential benefit rather than a threat. They saw Communism as a greater evil than Nazism, and cited Stalin's vicious purges as proof ... The Foreign Office, especially Sir Robert Vansittart at its head, warned against Hitler's ambition, but in vain. The government never decided which way it would turn ... Britain turned to the League and was disillusioned, looked at France and was looked back at with suspicious eyes, looked to Germany and was treated with flattery, respect and politeness.

Martin Gilbert, Britain and Germany Between the Wars *(1964).*

2   Write a summary of this passage in your own words, picking out the four points that you think are the most important.

It was Hitler who was breaking the Treaty of Locarno, although he had undertaken more than once to observe it. His military advisers were opposed to ill-prepared amateurish German soldiers being sent into the hitherto de-militarised zone. The friction between Paris and London over the Abyssinian war, however, made this an irresistible moment for Hitler to take the risk: perhaps he knew with his sixth sense that British popular opinion, being incensed against Mussolini, would be lenient towards Hitler's 'moving troops about in his own country', and it was impossible for Eden, now British Foreign Secretary in succession to Hoare, to convey to the public the menace and the treachery involved in Hitler's actions.

Elizabeth Wiskemann, Europe of the Dictators 1919–45 *(1966).*

3   For each of the two passages, sum up the author's argument in no more than two sentences.
Which passage did you find easier to summarise?

INTERPRETING THE EVIDENCE

No matter what issue you choose, you will discover that the evidence does not support only one possible interpretation. This is because History is about the lives of real people, who do not always agree with each other and whose actions arise from complex motives.

If you find that hard to accept, think of the last time you had a difficult decision to make. Suppose several of your friends want you to go to a concert with them, but on the same day your parents plan to visit relatives, some other friends invite you to a party and your neighbours offer to pay you to do some work in their garden. You have also bought a new computer game that you want to try out. Before making your decision you have many things to consider, from your own wishes to a need for money or a wish to avoid offending friends or relatives. When you make up your mind, different people might have different opinions about your reasons – and *your* version of your reasons might be different again! Whether any one of the others involved agrees with your decision may depend on how the decision affects them or on their attitude towards you in the first place.

If that is the case with a decision taken by one person on how to spend one day, explanations of historical events are likely to be even more open to a range of interpretations. As mentioned above, historians are always disagreeing about how to interpret the past, their views depending on their own beliefs and attitudes, on the detailed evidence they have studied and on their selection from that evidence. Their interpretations are also affected by new research which reveals more knowledge on which to base judgements.

Here is one illustration of how historians' interpretations change. Even today, the popular image of life in Britain in the 1930s is that of the depression, summed up in mass unemployment, the Means Test and the Jarrow Marches. At one time, this also represented the accepted historical interpretation of the period, most historians agreeing that the experience of the '30s was one of total gloom and misery. It is not hard to find evidence of this. Many photographers took pictures of unemployed miners and shipyard workers, newsreels survive which show vividly the misery of those who suffered, and there are many writings from the time, such as George Orwell's *The Road to Wigan Pier*, illustrating this side of British life. This picture is supported further by cold statistical evidence of unemployment in certain parts of Britain.

So strong was this image that when some historians began to suggest it did not show the whole picture people became very angry with them. I was a member of a class at Glasgow University which could not believe it when our lecturer, Dr Derek Aldcroft, told us that for most British people the 1930s were years of rising living standards. We told him this was nonsense, because of the high unemployment rates and the desperate poverty of places like Clydeside and the Newcastle area. His response was to point out that such conditions were confined to those parts of Britain which had depended on the old heavy industries: coal, iron and steel, shipbuilding. Other parts of the country were prosperous, especially the areas of the Midlands and south of England which benefited from the factories which produced the new consumer goods such as cars, radios and washing machines. He showed us evidence that wages in these areas actually rose while prices were falling and that labour-saving goods made life easier and more pleasant. In fact, he argued, more people gained than lost during this period, so his 'optimistic' interpretation was more accurate than the traditional 'pessimistic' interpretation.

You may think, as the class did at the time, that it is unfair to appear to ignore the sufferings of the unemployed. Dr Aldcroft would reply that it is just as unfair to paint a gloomy picture of the whole of Britain because of the bad conditions in some parts of the country. His views, which provoked a great deal of debate, had developed because of new research into areas which previous historians had ignored. That did not necessarily make them right, but because they were based on real evidence they were worthy of respect and examination.

Each person – you included – must balance the evidence and reach their own conclusion about this or any historical issue. And your conclusion can be as valid as mine or that of any professional historian. What matters is your ability to justify it by considering the evidence and giving sensible reasons for your opinion.

DEVELOPING YOUR PLAN

As your research progresses, you will learn about the factors involved in your chosen issue in more detail than is possible in your basic course work. This in turn will deepen your understanding of the issue itself and may change your interpretation of it, because you now have more information on which to base an opinion.

This changing knowledge, and perhaps interpretation, will be reflected in changes to your plan. These changes are likely to be at two levels.

- You may change the factors you identified originally as being important, by adding new ones, removing ones you no longer consider important or changing the way you have phrased them.
- You can now use these factors as headings under which to organise the evidence you have gathered. If you have found out a lot, this may mean you have to take decisions about which evidence is important enough to include and which can be left out. This process of selecting evidence is one which all historians must use, especially when they have a limited space or time in which to write up the results of their research.

It is worth spending a little time on developing the plan in this way, because it helps you to organise your thoughts and will provide a good guide to areas requiring more research. Again, at this stage, your teacher will be able to give you good advice about how to arrange your information most effectively.

By the time you have completed all the research you have time for, you should be able to create a final version of your plan, which will be the basis of the essay you write under examination conditions. This plan must not be more than 200 words long, so you should give some thought to the use you want to make of it.

Some people regard the plan as simply a store for all the information they have found out. Their plans contain lists of facts, with no attempt to organise these to support an argument. Such plans do not help them to write well-structured essays which consider the chosen issue, balance the evidence and reach a conclusion. Yours should be written in a way that will help you to do these things.

No format is ideal for everyone, but all plans should follow certain principles:

- Your plan must help you to argue a case. To do so convincingly, your ideas must be presented in a logical sequence. Your plan should include the main factors relating to your issue, in the order in which you want to discuss them.

- Your plan should free you from the worry of forgetting pieces of evidence that you want to include. Beside or beneath each of your factors, note the information you have chosen to support your point.
- Your plan must give an indication of how you are going to introduce your essay and what conclusion you will reach.

You may also decide to use some of your 200 words to remind yourself of any quotations you want to use, such as a particularly well-phrased summary of an historian's argument. If so, be careful that it does not take up more words than you can afford. Even if this is not the case, it is wise to save words by writing in note form, not in sentences.

4 Suppose you were preparing to write an essay about my earlier issue:

How justified was the British Government in following a policy of appeasement between 1936 and 1939?

Here are ten pieces of information that might be relevant to this issue. Decide which pieces of evidence should go with each of the five factors listed above, and make a note of each in the smallest number of words that would help you to remember it.

1 The East Fulham by-election of 1933 was won by a Labour Party candidate who was believed to be a pacifist.
2 Several prominent British politicians were very impressed by Hitler. The former Prime Minister, David Lloyd George, who met Hitler in 1936, returned to Britain to describe him as a man of supreme quality. The Labour MP and former party leader George Lansbury, who was a pacifist, wrote in 1937 that Hitler would not go to war unless other people pushed him into it.
3 Speaking in London in March 1936, the French Foreign Minister told his audience that the German reoccupation of the Rhineland had to be resisted by force or else growing German power would lead to war.
4 In 1938 several countries in the British Empire, including Canada and South Africa, said that they would not go to war in support of Britain should war break out with Germany over Czechoslovakia.
5 In a debate in the House of Commons in March 1936, Sir Winston Churchill warned that the atmosphere in Europe had changed recently to the extent that war was being regarded as a serious possibility. He also described the German occupation of the Rhineland as a menace to Holland, Belgium and France.
6 In 1935 the League of Nations Union organised a survey which has been nicknamed the 'Peace Ballot'. The historian AJP Taylor challenged the view that it showed the British people as determined to avoid

war at any price, pointing out that 6.75 million people out of the 11.5 million who gave their opinions said that war should be used to stop an aggressor.

7   Following the Munich agreement of September 1938, Duff Cooper resigned from his position as First Lord of the Admiralty, saying in the Commons that in his opinion the only way to deal with Hitler was to resist him by force.

8   When Chamberlain arrived at Heston aerodrome from Munich, waving his 'piece of paper' and talking of 'peace in our time', he was greeted by cheering crowds who regarded him as a hero for having prevented war.

9   In 1937 British experts estimated that a German air assault on Britain would last for 60 days, kill 600 000 people and injure another 1 200 000.

10 Many British politicians regarded Communism as a greater threat than Nazi Germany. Their view of brutal Communists was reinforced by the show trials of the 1930s in Stalin's Soviet Union.

My version of what this part of a plan might look like can be found on pages 14–15.

If you organise all of your chosen evidence in this way, your plan will have a structure that will be reflected in the essay itself. You should now be ready to write your essay with confidence, using the writing skills you have been developing for the essay section of the examination.

SOLUTIONS TO TASKS

Let us look at each of these questions and see what help they are to you.

1   Not very helpful. All you have to do is describe the work of Mrs Pankhurst. There is no real issue to analyse or evaluate, so you are unlikely to write an essay that is worth a good mark.

2   This is even worse. There is no question here at all, so it would be very difficult to know what information would be useful. As for coming to a conclusion, what would it be about?

3   Much more helpful. This question asks you to evaluate the work of the WSPU and compare it to other factors which helped women to gain the vote before coming to a conclusion about the relative importance of the WSPU.

4   Also a good – and challenging – question. Here you must decide what you would regard as success for the suffragette movement, balance the arguments for and against judging it as successful and then reach a conclusion one way or the other.

5 Another bad issue, asking only for a description. It does not encourage, or even allow, you to show your skills of evaluation and argument.

In fact, none of these is ideal, but a comparison of their demands may surprise you.

1 Although the awkward phrasing makes this question look complicated, actually it is the easiest of the three to research and write. It deals with one issue – why the Nazis were able to come to power – and asks you to compare five important factors. Probably you would want to consider all of these in any essay on the rise of Hitler, so this awkward looking question actually guides your research and helps you plan your essay.

2 A superb question – for a third year university student! You do not have time to research the intricate politics of the months before January 1933. In any case, you might find the issues much too complex given the normal depth of your historical study.

3 Deceptively simple looking – but disastrous. These are really two issues linked by the use of the word 'and':
   a) reasons for the Nazi achievement of power
   b) reasons why they were able to stay in power.
   You cannot do justice to both in one researched essay, even in two hours.

One way of connecting the information to your headings (which have been shortened to save a few words) might be as shown below. Notice that it is not possible to write down everything about each of the pieces of information. The words I have used are intended to act as prompts for the memory – even in the Extended Essay you still have to learn some of the facts you want to use as evidence!

* British public opinion:
  – East Fulham by-election
  – 'Peace Ballot': Taylor – 6.75 million for war to stop aggression
  – welcome for Chamberlain after Munich
* Politicians' views on Fascism/Communism:
  – Lloyd George on Hitler
  – Churchill: Rhineland reoccupation a menace to France, Belgium, Holland
  – Communism more dangerous than Nazism
  – Duff Cooper's resignation
* Economic depression
* Fear of bombing:

      – experts: 60 days; 600 000 dead; 1.2 million injured
- Policies of allies:
      – 1936 France for force over Rhineland
      – 1938 Empire countries would not support war

Notice that there are more points for some headings than for others. The economic depression has none at all. More research indicated there!

SECTION 2

Essay Writing

EXTENDED ESSAYS AND EXAMINATION ESSAYS

Everything that is suggested in this section applies equally to writing an essay under examination conditions and to the Extended Essay. Although you have longer in which to write the Extended Essay and have access to your prepared plan, the examiner will be looking for the same qualities in each – historical knowledge and understanding, analysis of the issue, the use of evidence and the ability to draw a conclusion. You will be able to include much more detail in the Extended Essay than is possible in the examination, but that should not mean that you simply cram in as much information as possible. Doing that alone will not gain you a better grade.

An essay which displays the qualities of a C pass essay in the examination but is 'beefed up' with extra detail is still a C pass essay; perhaps a better C but still a C. While essays worth A or B grades often contain more information, what distinguishes them is the way in which they use this information to discuss, argue, analyse and reach conclusions. Always keep this in mind.

Analysing the Question

Before you can write, or even plan, your essay you must read the question carefully. This may seem obvious, but many people do not take the trouble to do so. They appear to do little more than glance at it to get a rough idea of the theme – is it about women's rights movements, or trade unions, or the unification of Germany or Italy, or the Bolshevik Revolution of 1917? There is little concern about the issue raised in the question.

Those who do this are so eager to show off the facts they have learned that they give up the chance to demonstrate their skills as well. Their answers become narrative or descriptive, often concentrating almost totally on telling the story, with no attempt at historical discussion except, perhaps, briefly at the end.

But a History essay, like a discursive essay in English, asks you to do more than just tell the story. For instance, it may require you to weigh up the evidence for and against an argument, or compare the relative importance of factors in causing a particular event to take place. This makes it critical that, before you start, you ask the most important question of all –

*what does the question ask me to **do**?*

Here are some examples of styles of question that may crop up in Higher History examinations. What does each of these ask you to do?

THE DIRECT QUESTION

The simplest style of question is one in which you are asked quite directly to explain a historical event. This can be phrased in several ways:

Why did Russia fail to establish a democracy in 1917? (1992)

*Account for the growth of nationalism in **either** Germany **or** Italy between 1815 and 1850. (1994)*

Explain why the Scottish National Party did not achieve more electoral success between 1935 and 1979. (1992)

Although these questions may seem to ask you to describe a process or tell a story, it is impossible to do so without comparing the impact of a number of things which influenced the historical event or process. To take the first example, there was no one reason for the failure to set up a democracy in Russia. Among other things, that failure was caused by the absence of a democratic tradition in Tsarist Russia, by the effects of the First World War, by the collapse of the economy, by the weakness of the Kerensky Government and by the determination and organisation of the Bolsheviks under Lenin. To answer this question properly, it is necessary to consider what part each of these played in the failure of democracy in 1917 and then to reach a conclusion.

1 Here are some examples of questions of this type. For each one, from the sections you are studying, identify four factors whose importance you might consider in order to answer the question fully.

Section (a): Britain 1850s–1979
1 *Explain why the franchise in Britain was widened during the period 1850–1928.*

Section (b): The Growth of Nationalism
2 *What factors allowed the Nazis to stay in power in Germany between 1933 and 1939 **or** Mussolini to stay in power in Italy between 1923 and 1939?*

Section (c): The Large Scale State
3 *For what reasons did the economy of the USA suffer depression in the early 1930s?*
4 *Why were revolutionary movements in Russia unable to challenge Tsarist authority successfully in the years before 1905?*

At the end of this section you will find lists of possible factors with which to compare yours. These are not the 'right' answers, but simply suggestions of themes which could help to answer these questions.

QUESTIONS WHICH ASK YOU TO EVALUATE A TREND

Because it can cover long periods of time, the kind of question which deals with a historical trend appears most often in Section (a), Britain 1850s–1979, of the examination.

Consider again question 1 (shown in Task 1), taken from the British section of the course:

Explain why the franchise in Britain was widened during the period 1850–1928.

In this case, a good introduction might place the issue in context by giving a brief outline of how far the franchise was extended during this period before showing that the writer knows there were several reasons for this extension. This would allow the next stage in the essay, the development, to follow naturally by picking up a theme mentioned at the end of the introduction. Such an introduction could be two paragraphs long. It might read like this:

> In the 1850s, despite the Reform Act of 1832, only a tiny proportion of the British population had the right to vote. To gain this right, it was necessary to own a property worth £2 a year in rent, and to be a man. By 1928, when women were given the franchise on the same terms as men, almost every person over the age of 21 could vote.

> This process of extending the franchise took place in several stages, each of them giving new groups the right to vote for different reasons. By the 1860s, when radical campaigns for Parliamentary reform began again, 15 years after the collapse of Chartism, the voting population had increased simply because prosperity had given more people the wealth to meet the property qualifications. By then it was also clear that the 1832 Act had not caused the revolution which its opponents had predicted. Some politicians began to think that it was safe to expand the suffrage further.

The development of the answer could then begin with a discussion of the process that led up to the Second Reform Act of 1867. This question takes a theme, like the growth of democracy, and asks you to evaluate how far it changed over a particular period. Another very popular example, from the 1993 paper was:

To what extent had democracy been achieved in Britain by 1900?

To answer a question like this it is necessary first to define your terms. In this case, what makes a country a democracy? Is it simply the proportion of the population which is eligible to vote? Clearly not. Other issues are also important, like having a choice between parties which have different policies, or safety from intimidation or corruption through being able to vote secretly. You can add your own choice of criteria. Having done so, you must then consider what changes took place in Britain, by using the date given in the question as a guide, then evaluate how much closer these factors brought this country to fulfilling your criteria for a democracy. Which ones could now be said to have been met? Which ones remained to be met? Only then can you draw a conclusion about how close Britain was to being a democracy in 1900.

As with all questions, when evaluating a trend you should note carefully any cut-off date given, as it could affect your conclusion. In this case, the choice of the year 1900 means that your conclusion must reflect the fact that women had not yet received the vote. By then, the campaign for women's suffrage had not even received the kind of public attention that would come with the more dramatic activities of the Women's Social and Political Union. Had the question referred to 1918 or 1928, you would have to include the results of the Acts of those years and the part they played in extending the franchise to women.

THE CLUE OF THE ISOLATED FACTOR

You may be asked to compare the importance of different factors involved in a historical process. Usually, this kind of question will highlight one of the factors for you, giving you a clue about where to start. Here is a typical example; Option C, question 6, from the 1994 paper.

> *Assess the contribution of* **either** *Bismarck in Germany* **or** *Cavour in Italy to national unification.*

For the sake of this example I'll deal with Germany.

The usual mistake with this kind of question is to concentrate exclusively on the person or factor mentioned in the question. The effect can be something like this:

> 'Once upon a time there was a man called Bismarck and he became Minister-President in Prussia and he decided to unify Germany and he did it by fighting a series of wars. First there was the war with Denmark . . .'

Of course, I exaggerate, but only in the style of writing. This kind of story-telling approach is very common.

What does the question really ask? Its intention is to test your understanding of how the unification came about, so effectively you can split it into two parts, a general question and a direct instruction:

> *Assess the contribution of Bismarck in Germany to national unification*

becomes a question:

> *What factors brought about national unification in Germany?*

and an instruction:

> *Pay special attention to the contribution of Bismarck.*

To answer the question you would explain the importance of Bismarck's work in unifying Germany, but you would also compare his work with other factors such as growing nationalism in Germany, the expansion of Prussian economic and military power and the part played by foreign countries, like Italy and France, in the story.

You can recognise questions of this kind quite easily by the clue that they isolate one of a range of factors and by their use of certain phrases. The question discussed above might have been phrased in one of these ways:

How important was Bismarck's contribution to German unification?

or

To what extent was Bismarck responsible for German unification?

or

How far was German unification made possible by the increase in Prussian economic power?

This last question puts the emphasis on another factor, but still tests your understanding of the same theme.

Here are some more examples of questions of this type from recent papers. Try your own analysis by breaking each one down into a question and an instruction.

1   *To what extent were the social reforms of the Liberal Government (1906–14) prompted by feelings of genuine concern for the masses? (1992)*
2   *How far can the popularity of Scottish nationalism be attributed to economic discontent during the period 1930–79? (1991)*
3   *How important was the Ku Klux Klan in delaying the granting of civil rights to black Americans?*
4   *How far did the policies of the Tsarist Government contribute to the outbreak of revolution in 1905? (1993)*

Now compare your answers with my analyses of these questions on pages 38–39.

THE QUOTATION

You may be given a quotation and asked if you agree with it. This can be phrased in several ways, but they really all mean the same thing: *Discuss this view..., How far do you accept this assessment..., To what extent do you agree...?* Questions of this sort ask you to weigh up the evidence *for* and *against* the statement, and come to a conclusion.

For example, Option C, question 2, 1993.

'Between 1906 and 1914 the real causes of poverty were tackled successfully by government action.' To what extent would you agree with this statement?

Some might take this question as an invitation to catalogue the reforms of the Liberal Government: the Children's Charter, Old Age Pensions, Labour

Exchanges and the rest, described in detail but to no final purpose. Look more closely at the statement:

'Between 1906 and 1914 the real causes of poverty were tackled successfully by government action.'

What is the first thing you have to do before you can agree or disagree with this statement? You must say what the real causes of poverty were. You should have plenty of evidence for this in your studies of, for instance, the work of Seebohm Rowntree or Charles Booth. Once you have identified disease, old age and un-employment as being among the causes you can go on to consider the work of the Liberals in these areas, and decide whether or not you think the government's actions tackled these *successfully.*

As you can see, the information about the reforms of the Liberal Government is not wrong or irrelevant. In fact, it is central to a good answer, because it provides the foundation for a proper discussion of the issue, but these factors must be used to help you justify your argument.

A quotation can also be another form of the Clue of the Isolated Factor (see page 20). Within the quotation the writer asserts that a particular factor is the most important in explaining a historical event or process, and you are asked to assess how accurate the quotation is. In the case of the question on Bismarck and German unification (see page 20), the question might read:

'The work of Bismarck was the most significant cause of German unification.' To what extent do you accept this judgement?

Although phrased as a statement, what you have to do is still the same: show an understanding of all the causes of German unification, pay special attention to Bismarck's work and draw a conclusion about the significance of his work by comparison with the other factors you have identified.

③ Here are some examples of quotations of this type. For each one, identify what you have to do before you can agree or disagree with the statement. Try it even if it refers to a topic you have not studied – for this task you don't actually have to know about the topic!

1   *Twentieth-century peace movements have all been unsuccessful in achiev-ing their aims.*
2   *The Nazi achievement of power in Germany was, more than anything else, due to their promise to overthrow Versailles.*
3   *Black radical protest movements in the USA during the 1960s did more harm than good to the campaign for civil rights.*
4   *In the end, Tsar Nicholas II of Russia was responsible for his own downfall.*

You can find my answers for comparison on page 39.

PLANNING YOUR ESSAY

Once you have worked out what the question is asking you to do, the next step is to organise your information. It can be very tempting, especially if you know a lot about a particular topic, to start at the beginning and try to tell the whole story – as a story. Although this approach tells the examiner you have learned plenty of facts, it does not show your understanding of the issue. In other words, it does not help you to answer the question asked.

Suppose you have decided to answer the question discussed earlier:

> *Assess the contribution of **either** Bismarck in Germany **or** Cavour in Italy to national unification.*

Many candidates give in to the temptation to 'say all you know about' Bismarck or Cavour. At its simplest this leads to answers whose outlines look something like this:

Bismarck	Cavour
Bismarck becomes Minister-President of Prussia.	Cavour becomes Prime Minister of Piedmont.
Bismarck overcomes liberal opposition to increased taxation to pay for army reforms.	Cavour introduces economic and transport reforms.
Bismarck engineers Danish war over Schleswig and Holstein.	Cavour gains support of Napoleon III at Plombières.
Bismarck isolates and defeats Austria, forming the North German Confederation.	Cavour, with French support, provokes Austria into war, resulting in the gain of Lombardy.
Bismarck provokes war with France by doctoring the Ems telegram.	Cavour turns a blind eye to the departure of Garibaldi for Sicily.
Prussia defeats France and the German Empire is declared. So Bismarck's personal contribution to German unification was very important.	Cavour accepts Naples and Sicily for Victor Emmanuel and most of Italy is united. So Cavour's personal contribution to Italian unification was very important.

While understandable, these approaches do not lead to good essays which do what the question asks you to do. If you have analysed the question, you will know that it asks you to compare the work of Bismarck or Cavour with the other factors involved and to draw a conclusion from the evidence you present.

To do this effectively, your essay must divide into three sections, each of which has an important part to play. These are the Introduction, the Development and the Conclusion.

The Introduction

There was once an examiner in a Higher English examination who opened an essay paper to find, as the first words in the script, 'By the time you read this I shall be dead.' I don't know what the examiner thought of the rest of the essay, but I am certain that the opening sentence grabbed his or her attention pretty forcefully. It turned out that these words were not a suicide statement by the candidate but the opening words of a letter written to the narrator of a short story, but undoubtedly they had the intended effect – to make the examiner sit up!

Although you are unlikely to have the opportunity for as dramatic an opening line as that, the introduction is your chance to seize the examiner's attention. A good introduction can transmit a very powerful impression which may last even if the main part of your essay doesn't quite match it. Remember, the examiner will be reading over 200 scripts, many of which include answers on the most popular topics. Large numbers of these will be routine – the examiner may even be feeling a little bored by reading much the same thing, script after script. So, if you can, try to begin with an introduction that does three vital things:

- it shows you know what the question is about and what it has asked you to do;
- it does so in a lively and interesting manner and, if appropriate, perhaps even a dramatic way;
- it gives you a natural entry into the development stage of the essay.

Compare these two opening paragraphs in answers to the question on Bismarck's contribution to the unification of Germany:

1 The contribution of Bismarck was very important in helping to bring about the unification of Germany. Other factors like the Zollverein and nationalism were also important. To judge how important Bismarck's contribution was it is necessary to compare it with these other factors.

2 When Otto von Bismarck was recalled from Paris to become Minister-President of Prussia in 1862, German nationalism was already more than 40 years old. First apparent in the opposition to Napoleon's occupation of the German states, national feeling grew into a movement after 1815. This feeling was encouraged by a growth of interest in German literature and music and by increased economic cooperation between the north German states. By 1848 it was strong enough to make the creation of a united Germany one of the main demands of the revolutionaries.

Which one is more interesting to read? Both are sound introductions which show that the writer is aware of the need to mention more than Bismarck to answer the question thoroughly; that is, to place the issue in its broader context. The first one, though, simply says there are other factors to be considered, while the second connects these to each other and to the issue in a way that suggests deeper understanding. The examiner is impressed, and now expects to read a good, well-informed and argued essay.

One pitfall to avoid in writing your introduction is beginning with a conclusion, by expressing an opinion on the issue in the first sentence, like:

> 'The most important reason for variations in the popularity of Scottish nationalism is . . .'

or

> 'I agree/disagree with the view in the quotation that . . .'

This practice is not helpful for several reasons. Firstly, it gives away your argument too early, before you have displayed and evaluated the evidence. Secondly, for this reason it forces you to present your evidence in a way that supports your original statement, perhaps leading you to omit inconvenient evidence or to ignore opposing arguments instead of considering them properly. Finally, and most dangerous of all, by the time you reach your conclusion the evidence you present may lead you to change your mind!

TO SUM UP

In your introduction:

1 Set out clearly the issue raised in the question to show that you understand what you have to do.

2 Identify the main themes you intend to deal with in the rest of the essay.

3 Try to create a natural link to the development section.

4 Make a special effort to write in an interesting way that will attract the examiner's attention, if you can do so without making it seem artificial.

4

Look at question 1 from Task 2:

To what extent were the social reforms of the Liberal Government (1906–1914) prompted by feelings of genuine concern for the masses?

---

1 What information might you give in your introduction about the Liberal social reforms in order to place your answer in context?

2 Give three factors, apart from 'feelings of genuine concern for the masses', that you could mention in your introduction to show your awareness of the need for comparisons in your answer.

3 Write a paragraph, including this information, which would achieve

these purposes and give you a natural starting point for your development.

You can find a possible way of doing this on pages 39–40.

Practice Section 1

A. Analyse the questions from this list which relate to the sections of the course you are studying. What does each one ask you to do?

1   How important a part did the Labour Movement play in changing Britain's political identity between 1880 and 1924?
2   'Violent action was the main cause of the extension of the franchise between 1860 and 1920.' How far do you agree with this judgement?
3   How well did the policies of the National Government (1931–40) solve the problems of mass unemployment and Depression?
4   'The popularity of Scottish nationalism has always depended on the economic conditions at the time.' To what extent do you accept this view of the period 1930–1979?
5   How important were nationalist feelings in explaining why Germany **or** Italy became united?
6   Why did the Weimar Republic in Germany fail?
or   How successfully did Mussolini solve Italy's domestic problems between 1922 and 1939?
7   To what extent did black Americans achieve equal rights by 1968?
8   Explain the success of the Bolshevik Revolution in Russia in October 1917.
9   How far did the ideas of Sun Zhongsan (Sun Yat-sen) influence the rule of Jiang Jieshi (Chiang Kai-shek) in China?

B. Choose three of the above questions and write an introductory paragraph which shows clearly that you understand the issue in the question and which gives you a natural starting point for the development section of the essay.

The Development of Your Essay

As its name suggests, this is the section of your essay in which you develop your argument, using the information you have learned (your evidence) to expand on your basic points. It is also the section of the essay where there is the greatest temptation to lapse into narrative or descriptive writing, in your eagerness to show off the range of your knowledge.

Try to remember that the History course is designed to do more than fill your head with facts about the past. Of course, it is intended that you learn historical facts, but not to learn them uselessly, like so many pieces of trivia. You are also expected to learn how to make judgements about events, to weigh up evidence and draw conclusions – to evaluate. The most important factor which will persuade an examiner to give you a high grade is quality of thought. The examiner will certainly expect you to present a reasonable quantity of evidence, but will be even more interested in how you use that evidence.

- Is the evidence relevant to the issue in the question?
- Are the main points presented in a logical order?
- Is the evidence used to illustrate or develop points in the argument?
- Is there a sign that the writer is aware of possible alternative interpretations of the evidence?

ORGANISING YOUR EVIDENCE

If you have analysed the question accurately and identified the main factors to evaluate, the organisation of your evidence should be quite straightforward.

Suppose you decide to answer the question:

How important a contribution did Socialist societies make to the formation of the Labour Party?

Your analysis reveals that you need to compare the various factors which led to the formation of the Labour Party, paying special attention to the Socialist societies. You decide to consider three other factors: the growth of the Trade Unions, the extension of the franchise to working-class people and the failure of other parties to address the problems of the working classes. This is made clear in your introduction.

Each of these four factors should now have a section of its own, perhaps a single paragraph or, if necessary, two or three. In this way, information which is related is kept together, giving shape to the essay and providing a natural flow of ideas.

It would still be easy, even after this preparation, to drift into a description of each of the factors in the desire to show your knowledge of the facts. The result would be an account of the beliefs of the Social Democratic Federation and the Fabian Society, followed by an outline of the growth of New Unionism and the dramatic story of the Match Girls' Strike or the 1889 Dock Strike. However, in what way would even an accurate and lively narrative of this sort help to answer the question? It is important to show what part each one played in the creation of the Labour Party. Your knowledge is still displayed, but now it works for you, contributing to your discussion, like this:

- the Socialist societies gave the Labour Party some of its basic beliefs, such as public ownership of industry and transport;
- the extension of the franchise created a large number of working-class voters, especially in industrial towns and cities, many of whom came to believe that they needed a party of their own to represent their interests;
- in the late nineteenth century, Liberal and Conservative governments seemed to have other priorities, such as Ireland or foreign policy;
- the New Unions, whose members included many unskilled and low-paid workers, had the ability to support the new party financially and also provided many of its early leaders.

In each paragraph of your development, one of these points forms the main theme, which is illustrated and developed through your detailed knowledge.

If the question is of a different type, asking you to weigh up arguments for and against a viewpoint, the same principle still applies. Consider this question:

Did the activities of women's rights movements help or hinder the cause of women's suffrage before 1914?

Although you need to know what the activities of women's rights movements were during this period, once again it is not sufficient simply to describe them. You must explain the arguments for regarding them as helping and hindering their cause, so that you can reach a balanced conclusion. Some of the points you might make could include the following.

- The non-violent campaigns of the National Union of Women's Suffrage Societies persuaded a number of Members of Parliament to support giving women the vote. Several of them introduced private members' Bills to do so even before 1900. This suggests that such methods helped the cause of women's suffrage.

But
- None of these Bills were successful and by the early 1900s it seemed un-likely that these methods alone would convince Parliament to vote for women's suffrage. This suggests that peaceful methods, even if they did not actually hinder the cause, would not work, at least in the short term.
- The increasingly violent methods used by the Women's Social and Political Union gained the cause enormous publicity and made the issue a focus for political debate. This suggests that these methods helped to-wards the achievement of votes for women.

But
- These methods led many people (including some women) to argue that the women who carried out acts of violence were irresponsible, and

therefore did not deserve the vote. This suggests that they may have hindered progress towards their goal of equal suffrage.

As in the previous example, your detailed knowledge is used to illustrate and expand the points being made. You could give a few instances of the methods used by suffragist and suffragette groups, or of individuals who criticised the violent tactics of Christabel Pankhurst and her followers. The knowledge is valuable, but not for its own sake. It is valuable because it allows you to explain your argument more deeply, using precise examples in order to strengthen a point.

5 In the examination you meet the question:

'The welfare reforms of the Labour Government of 1945–51 were successful in meeting the needs of the British people.' Do you agree?

In the introduction you have set the issue in context by identifying the 'five giants' of want, ignorance, idleness, disease and squalor, named in the Beveridge Report as the main enemies of the British people. You have claimed that, in order to meet the needs of the people, the government had to defeat these 'five giants'.

From your learning, you have isolated these main points that you want to include in your answer:

- the extension of the National Insurance scheme to provide new benefits for people who were elderly, unemployed or ill;
- the building of new houses to replace those destroyed in the war and to improve the quality of housing in working-class areas;
- the introduction of the National Health Service in 1948;
- the encouragement of full employment;
- the setting up of Grammar Schools and Secondary Modern Schools.

These are only headings. For each one:

- Say whether or not you think it was successful in meeting the needs of the people in that area, giving a reason for your opinion;
- Give two or three examples of detailed information that could be used to illustrate your argument.

You may wish to compare your answers with my ideas on pages 40–41.

IN GOOD ORDER

To get the maximum value from your knowledge, it is worth giving some thought to the order in which you present it. If this is done effectively, it shows that you have a good understanding of the issue raised in the question and of how various factors interact to explain it.

If your argument deals with four main themes, it is most unlikely that they will all be of equal importance. To begin with, the question may require you to 'pay special attention' to one of them. Then again, you may have more information about some factors than about others, or may intend to conclude that one particular factor is the most important.

In your mind, or on paper if you prefer, list the four themes in order of importance. If you were answering the question on the Socialist societies and the formation of the Labour Party, it might look like this:

1   The contribution of the socialist societies – most important to deal with because the question refers to it.
2   The Trade Union movement – very important because of their financial support.
3   The increase in working people who could vote – important but with less direct impact on the formation of the party.
4   The failures of the other parties – less important though helped to convince some people that a party for the working class was necessary.

What happens if you go through these in this order in the essay? Your points appear in descending order of importance. While you may still write a good essay, it loses some of its potential impact as its most powerful points are followed by less and less forceful ones. The structure of the essay is weaker than it could be, and your conclusion may appear to be tagged on at the end rather than arising naturally from a progression of the argument.

Once you have given the themes an order of importance, you can arrange them to maximise their effect. There are various ways to achieve this but, above all, the points should appear in a logical order, so that you can move naturally from one point to the next.

Where there can be more than one logical approach, as in the question above, you can put your points in an order which is designed to make the main themes stand out even further. Start with the second most important theme, which will still be strong enough to lead off your discussion. Then take the next two in descending order. Finally, when the reader is perhaps thinking that your argument is beginning to fade out, you finish with the theme, factor or argument that you regard as the strongest. In this way, your most powerful argument appears immediately before your conclusion, which should arise naturally from it. An essay structured in this way will carry more conviction and so will create a better impression than one which goes through the points like a shopping list, with little evident pattern to it.

Try prioritising an answer yourself. In the section of the examination on nationalism, you might find a question such as this;

To what extent were the weaknesses of the Weimar constitution responsible for the rise to power of the Nazi Party?

Obviously, you could make a long list of the factors that contributed to this process, but for this purpose say you choose just four:

- the weaknesses of the Weimar constitution;
- German reaction to the Treaty of Versailles;
- Nazi propaganda campaigns;
- the economic crises of 1922–23 and 1929–32.

Arrange these into the order which you think would be most effective in giving your essay a logical structure, giving reasons for putting each factor in a particular place. My ideas are given on page 41.

MAKING LINKS

The idea of a structure in an essay is helped still further by making links between the various factors, arguments and pieces of evidence to show how they relate to each other. This skill is perhaps the most subtle of all the essay writing skills, but its mastery pays rich rewards. There are two ways in which this technique can enhance an essay. Firstly, within a paragraph, it can be used to allow a piece of evidence to reinforce or illustrate a point. Secondly, it can be used to connect paragraphs, to show how their themes are linked, so giving a flow to the argument.

Take the question on the activities of women's rights movements (see page 28). While dealing with the work of the suffragists, you may wish to develop the idea that their methods were showing few signs of success by the early years of the twentieth century. Here are two ways in which similar information can be presented. In the first, the information is given, but is allowed to sit there without working. In effect, it is a narrative.

> The first organisations to campaign for votes for women were known as suffragists. They used peaceful methods like petitions, public meetings and sending letters to Members of Parliament. They claimed that more than half of the MPs had said they supported votes for women. By 1900 some of the MPs had put forward Bills to give women the vote, but these had all failed. Some women began to say that politicians would not do anything if they only used peaceful methods.

In this second version, a little extra detail is added to the evidence, and pieces of information are joined together to make a point.

> Despite over 30 years of campaigning since the formation of the early suffrage societies in the 1860s, the achievement of the vote seemed as distant as ever in 1900. Although the suffragists claimed that over half of the Members of Parliament had told them individually that they favoured votes for women, none of the private Bills of the 1880s and 1890s had succeeded. The more impatient of the women began to argue that the men in power would never give

priority to a cause promoted only by letters, speeches and petitions, even if nearly three million people had signed such petitions in only two years (1878–79).

In the second version, there is little extra information, but the way in which it is written helps it to be used more effectively. This is done by using simple linking words and phrases. A good example is the second sentence, which joins together the last two sentences of the first version by using the word 'although' to suggest a contrast between two facts – the suffragists' claim that over half of the current Members of Parliament had given them expressions of support and the failure of the various Bills to get through Parliament. This suggests to the examiner that the writer understands the connection more fully than is displayed in the first version. Notice also that the addition of a small amount of extra detail (the number of people who signed suffragist petitions over a two year period) adds extra weight to the point being made.

In every essay you write there are opportunities to create such links between pieces of evidence. There will also be chances to connect themes by using similar phrases at the beginning of a paragraph. Continuing with the example of women's rights movements, you want to link the two arguments over the value of the suffragette campaign of violence: that it raised the profile of the issue and that it turned some people against the campaign. The discussion of the first point might end like this:

> Actions like the smashing of the shop windows in London's West End, women chaining themselves to the railings outside the Houses of Parliament and Buckingham Palace, or the dramatic suicide of Emily Wilding Davison at the Derby in 1913, kept the cause in the headlines and ensured that the government could never forget the women's demands. They also demonstrated the depth of the women's determination to achieve their aims, reminding many that in 1832 and in 1867 violent actions by men had influenced Parliament to pass reform measures which increased the male franchise.

Instead of going on to say, at the start of the next paragraph, 'some people regarded acts of violence as irresponsible', a more definite link can be created like this:

> Valuable though this publicity was, some argued that the campaign of violence was actually damaging the cause by giving the impression that the militant suffragettes were irresponsible and so did not deserve the vote. Among these was Winston Churchill, who informed a deputation from the Women's Freedom League that their cause was 'marching backwards'.

Notice how the introductory phrase reflects back to the previous paragraph, helping to sustain continuity of thought and to add emphasis to the contrast between the two views of the suffragette actions.

In the section of the examination dealing with the Large Scale State, there might be a question asking:

How important was economic and social distress in causing the outbreak of revolution in Russia in 1905?

Among the factors leading to that outbreak of revolution, you could begin by considering living and working conditions in industrial towns, peasant grievances and the growth of revolutionary groups. In the next paragraph you should comment on the Russo-Japanese War. In a simple narrative account, that paragraph might begin:

In 1904, following tension over rivalry in Manchuria, Russia went to war with Japan after an attack on Port Arthur. Most people expected Russia to win the war easily, but instead the Japanese forces defeated the Russians, who suffered badly from difficulties in communication. This defeat contributed to the outbreak of revolution as it was a humiliation for Russia, for which the Tsar's government took the blame.

Now look at how the use of a short linking passage can transform this information from narrative to analysis:

If the social conditions in town and country created the unrest and the revolutionary societies supplied some of the ideas that could lead to revolution, the government's folly in being drawn into war with Japan provided the occasion. They hoped for a short, victorious war to restore their credibility and unite the country behind the Tsar. Instead, the war lasted over a year, showing up the inefficiency of the transport system, which crippled Russian supply routes, and of the military. The shock of a heavy defeat by a small nation brought only humiliation for the country and for its leaders, and encouraged revolutionaries to rise in protest.

Once more, the reference back to issues raised in previous paragraphs helps the continuity of the argument and suggests ways in which the various factors interacted with each other.

Here is a possible question on the topic of Scottish political identity:

'The main obstacle to Scottish devolution in the 1970s was the fear that it would raise taxes to an unacceptable level.' Do you agree?

Two of the ideas that you should discuss are the issue raised in the question, the tax implications of a devolved Scottish Parliament, and the 'West Lothian Question', of the voting powers of Scottish MPs in the United Kingdom Parliament.

Write a couple of sentences that could be used at the beginning of a paragraph, to lead the discussion from the first of these factors to the second. One way of doing this is shown on page 41.

Practice Section 2

A. Take the three questions from Practice Section 1 (see page 26) for which you wrote an introductory paragraph. Write down four main points that you should discuss in your development, together with some examples of detailed information that could be used to develop these points.

B. Write a paragraph about each of these points, showing its importance in discussing the issue raised in the question. As you do so, take care to show the links between each point and the others. Do this by putting connecting sentences at the beginning of each paragraph.

The Conclusion

A strong conclusion to your essay is as important as a strong introduction. It creates a good final impression with the examiner and confirms the quality of your understanding of the issue.

A good conclusion does two main jobs.

*   It summarises the main points in the argument.
*   It gives a direct answer to the question asked.

The last point is very important. Many conclusions restate the main points well enough but come to a stop without providing an answer to the question. To go back to the question on the effectiveness of the Liberal reforms of 1906–14 (see pages 20–21), such a conclusion could read:

> During the period 1906–14 the Liberals passed reforms to help remove some of the main causes of poverty. The health of children was dealt with through

free school meals and medical inspection in schools. The problems of elderly people were tackled through Old Age Pensions and poverty, caused by disease or unemployment, through National Insurance contributions. Some people say that these reforms were the first step towards the Welfare State.

The problem here is that this paragraph does not answer the question, which asked whether or not you agreed that government action tackled the real causes of poverty 'successfully'. It gives a summary list of some of the major reforms of the period, but does not discuss the issue of the success of these reforms. Much more impressive would be a conclusion like this, which keeps the question in mind:

> The reforms of the period 1906–14 were certainly targeted more closely at the causes of poverty, such as age, disease and unemployment, identified by researchers like Booth and Rowntree, than previous measures had been. It would, however, be an exaggeration to say that these were all tackled 'successfully', for much poverty remained after 1914. Some of the reforms, like free school meals, were not compulsory, while others, such as insurance against unemployment, only affected workers in a few industries. Even the Old Age Pension, welcome though it was, was set at a deliberately low level to encourage people to save for their old age. The Liberal reforms certainly brought about a great step forwards in the battle against poverty, but the battle remained to be won.

This version uses the phrasing of the question as its focus, using the summary of the reforms simply to illustrate the argument. It refers back to the causes of poverty and states an opinion about how successfully these were tackled by the reforms. In the last sentence, it gives a direct answer to the question, while avoiding the use of 'I agree …' or 'I disagree …', 'I think …' or 'In my opinion …', all of which are unnecessary and may be regarded as immature. It is much better to follow the practice of professional historians and state your opinions confidently as though they were facts. This remains true where the question asks for a comparison between various factors involved in an issue, as in the question on Bismarck and German Unification considered earlier (pages 20–25). Suppose your assessment is that Bismarck's contribution was the most important factor in the process of unification. A reasonable enough but routine conclusion might read:

> This evidence shows that there were many factors which helped to bring about German unification. These included growing national feeling in Germany, the increasing strength of Prussia and the efficiency of her army, and the errors made by other countries. Bismarck's contribution was the most important because he led Prussia in the victorious wars against Denmark, Austria and France which actually brought the German states together as a united country.

This does mention some of the main factors and does give an answer to the question. However, the factors other than Bismarck's contributions are just listed, without an explanation of what their impact was, while the reason given for choosing Bismarck as being the most important factor is a limited one. All it really says is that he was the leader when unification was achieved, therefore he made the most important contribution. With very little alteration, the same passage could have been used as an introduction.

Here is a more sophisticated approach, reaching the same conclusion but indicating not just which factors were involved but saying why they were important:

> The proclamation of the German Empire in 1871 was the climax of a long process, to which several factors contributed. The growth of nationalism brought about the demand for a united country. Prussian economic development, aided by the Zollverein, allowed the build up of its military power and strengthened its influence, at least among the northern states. Together, these developments made possible a unification under Prussian leadership, but they did not make it certain. What made Bismarck's contribution decisive was his ability to exploit this potential for unity and to overcome the barriers which still lay in the path of unification, especially the opposition of France and Austria. His diplomatic skills in isolating his enemies and his willingness to seize opportunities turned the possibility of unification into reality.

This longer version actually does what the question asks – it assesses Bismarck's contribution in the light of at least some other factors and concludes (though without using the actual word) that his contribution was the most important of all.

Of course, it is not necessary to conclude that the factor mentioned in a question is the most important. Remember that in a History essay there is no 'correct' answer. The examiners (who, being historians, are likely to hold differing opinions anyway!) must reward you for showing the skills being tested, whether or not they accept your conclusion. What matters is that your conclusion can be defended and that it arises from a proper evaluation of the evidence. Let's prove it.

8 Take the question about Bismarck (page 20) and write a conclusion which mentions the same factors but argues that the economic growth of Prussia, not Bismarck, was the most important factor in German unification. My version of such a conclusion is given on pages 41–42.

Where a question asks you to agree or disagree with a statement, your conclusion should balance the evidence for and against it. For instance, question 4 from Task 3 (see page 22) asks you if you agree with the statement:

> *'In the end, Tsar Nicholas II of Russia was responsible for his own downfall.'*

Here is one way in which the arguments for and against could be compared.

> Many excuses could be made in defence of the Tsar. It could be argued that he was the victim of an outdated system of governing Russia, which he could

hardly be expected to reform himself, especially with his upbringing and beliefs. Further, the shocking impact of the First World War on the Russian army and civilians cannot be blamed on the Tsar alone. On the other hand, his willingness to put so much faith in the appalling Rasputin and his failure to respond effectively to the crisis affecting his people turned away many who might have defended him. Nicholas II was not to blame personally for all of Russia's ills, but his errors during the critical months of late 1916 and early 1917 finally lost him the confidence of his people, his throne and eventually his life.

Notice how this conclusion recognises that there could be arguments in favour of different viewpoints before expressing a definite opinion on the question.

TO SUM UP

In your conclusion:

1 Summarise the main points in your argument, commenting on how each one relates to the issue raised in the question.

2 Make a decision about the issue, explaining why you have reached that conclusion.

Practice Section 3

A. Go back to the three questions you chose for Practice Sections 1 and 2. Write down three main points that you should include in your conclusion, with a brief note of how each relates to the issue raised in the question.
B. Write a concluding paragraph for each essay, explaining these points and giving a clear answer to the question. Try to show that you are aware that it could be possible to argue in favour of a different conclusion.

If you now put together your answers to the three Practice Sections, you should have at least the substantial outlines of three good essays in answer to your chosen questions.

SOLUTIONS TO TASKS

1 Reasons for the extension of the franchise in Britain 1850–1928:
   • Demands from reformers, e.g. radicals, Labour movement, suffragettes

- Changes in the British economy and society, e.g. industrial and urban growth
- Earlier reforms did not bring disaster – 1832
- Attitudes of politicians, e.g. Disraeli in 1867

2 Factors in keeping Nazis in power in Germany:
- Fear – concentration camps, SS, Gestapo
- Economic successes, e.g. reduction of unemployment
- Propaganda and indoctrination – Nuremberg rallies, press and radio
- Foreign policy achievements – rearmament, reoccupation of the Rhineland

Factors in keeping Fascists in power in Italy:
- Fear, e.g. murder of Matteotti
- Lack of effective alternative government
- Propaganda and indoctrination, e.g. Dopolavoro
- Foreign policy achievements, e.g. Abyssinia

3 Reasons for economic depression in the USA:
- Economic policies of Republican governments in the 1920s
- Over reliance on credit to provide prosperity in the 1920s
- Wall Street Crash of October 1929
- Effect of depression in other countries on world trade

4 Causes of inability of revolutionary movements to challenge Tsarist authority before 1905:
- Divisions among revolutionaries – different aims, methods
- Limited political awareness among the masses
- Repressive measures taken by the régime
- Influence of the Orthodox Church

1 **Question**
- What were the reasons for the passage of the Liberal social reforms?

Instruction
- Pay special attention to their feelings of concern for the masses.

2 **Question**
- What were the causes of the popularity of Scottish nationalism between 1930 and 1979?

Instruction
- Pay special attention to economic discontent.

3 **Question**
- What were the causes of the delay in granting civil rights to black Americans?

Instruction
- Pay special attention to the Ku Klux Klan.

4 **Question**
- What were the reasons for the outbreak of revolution in Russia in 1905?

Instruction
- Pay special attention to the policies of the Tsarist Government.

3

1 Identify the aims of twentieth-century peace movements.
Say what have been their achievements and their failures.
Compare these with their aims to assess the extent to which these have been achieved.

2 Explain the various reasons for the Nazi achievement of power.
Discuss in particular detail the importance of the promise to overthrow the treaty of Versailles.
Compare its importance with that of the other factors to reach a conclusion.

3 State what the activities of black radical protest movements were in the 1960s.
Identify ways in which they may be said to have helped the cause of civil rights.
Identify ways in which they may be said to have damaged the campaign for civil rights.
Compare these in order to reach a conclusion.

4 Identify the ways in which Nicholas II can be considered to have caused the Revolution of February 1917.
Explain what other factors helped to bring about that Revolution.
Compare the importance of all of the factors to assess how important his own part was.

1 The Liberal reforms of 1906–14 attempted to deal with the problems of children, the old, the sick and the unemployed. Their measures included medical inspection in schools, the Old Age Pension, National Health Insurance and setting up Labour Exchanges.

2 Factors inspiring these reforms included:
- 'New Liberalism' and a move away from *laissez-faire*;
- Concern about the physical state of the nation which might weaken Britain's ability to fight a war;
- The example of welfare measures abroad, especially in Germany;
- Competition from the Labour Party for the votes of working-class people.

3 At first sight the reforms of the Liberal Government of 1906–14 appear to have been passed in order to help the masses of people suffering from poverty. Measures like medical inspection in schools, National Health

Insurance, Labour Exchanges and the Old Age Pension seem designed to deal with some of the worst causes of poverty. Although this might suggest a government with 'genuine concern for the masses', there is evidence that this was not the only reason for passing these reforms.* Other influences included the fear that the health of the British people, especially in cities, had become so poor that Britain would find it difficult to raise a strong army in time of war, New Liberalism (which was leading some members of the government away from traditional *laissez-faire* ideas), the example of welfare laws in other countries and the Liberals' need to compete for votes with the rising Labour Party.

1 The National Insurance scheme was not completely successful, as some elderly people did not qualify for full pension benefits and the normal rate of unemployment benefit did not meet the needs of some people. However, the 'safety net' of National Assistance meant that almost everyone was entitled to help in time of trouble.

The government's housing policy was not very successful due to the high cost and scarcity of building materials after the war. There was still a serious housing shortage by 1951.

The National Health Service was very successful, despite some problems, because it gave everyone the right to free medical treatment at the point of use.

There were very low levels of unemployment during this period, but this had little to do with government policy and was caused much more by an increase in British exports and by post-war reconstruction which required a large amount of labour.

The education policy, in reality a legacy from the wartime Coalition government, was not successful, because the Secondary Modern Schools were seen as second-class schools, giving those who attended them an inferior education.

2 Here are some examples of detailed information that might be used to develop, illustrate or reinforce these factors. Note that these are by no means the only ones that could have been chosen.

National Insurance

Benefits which were provided included sickness and unemployment benefit, maternity grants, pensions and death grants. Family allowances

---

* Note: This paragraph is designed to show you a way of putting all these ideas together in the introduction. In this case, it would save time and space to start your development with a new paragraph after the asterisk. This could discuss why people had begun to fear that the health of the population was seriously weak – the investigations by Booth and Rowntree and the rejection of many recruits at the time of the Boer War on health grounds. The points made later in the paragraph would appear at the appropriate stage, later in the essay.

were paid direct to mothers as many people believed that fathers were likely to squander the money.

Housing

The rate of house building between 1946 and 1951 averaged only 150 000 a year, compared to over 350 000 a year in the period 1934–39.

Many people had to be given temporary accommodation in prefabricated houses.

National Health Service

The service was introduced in the face of strong opposition from the British Medical Association.

The popularity of the service (over five million pairs of spectacles being issued in the first year) meant that it cost much more than expected, forcing the government to introduce charges for spectacles and dental treatment.

Employment

The British share of the world's export trade in manufactured goods went up from 18.6 per cent in 1938 to 25.6 per cent in 1950.

One of the main reasons for this success was that two of Britain's pre-war trading rivals, Germany and Japan, were in no position to compete.

Education

To decide who went to the new types of school, an eleven-plus examination was introduced.

Many middle-class people did not trust the state school system and, if they could afford it, sent their children to independent schools.

There could be arguments in favour of putting this list of factors in almost any order. You could start with the weakness of Weimar because the constitution is mentioned in the question and it does come first chronologically, then move on to the reaction to Versailles, the economic crises and finally Nazi propaganda. Such an approach would be largely chronological, but the factors did react on each other so it would be easy to link them positively.

Alternatively, you could begin with Versailles, which created the anger that brought Hitler so much support. This could be followed by the economic crises, which depressed many people and made them vulnerable to the Nazi message. The power of Nazi propaganda to influence people could be taken next, before finishing with the argument that even these factors could not have allowed Hitler to reach power in isolation of the weaknesses of the Weimar constitution.

While the prospect of higher taxes was enough to turn some Scots against the proposal, others were worried about the constitutional implications, as raised in the 'West Lothian Question' by the Labour MP Tam Dalyell. If Scotland had its own Parliament to make decisions about Scottish affairs, why should Scottish MPs at Westminster be allowed to vote on matters concerning England?

 Bismarck did indeed make a large contribution to the achievement of German unification. His diplomatic skills allowed the Prussian army to defeat Austria and France without foreign interference, and his eye for an opportunity enabled these wars to take place at the best possible moments for Prussia. Yet he was fortunate enough to be in the position to complete a process which had been going on since national feelings had been aroused by the fight against Napoleon, leading to a demand for unification which had to be satisfied at some point anyway. Even more important were Prussia's economic and industrial growth, which gave it the ability to challenge Austria for leadership in Germany and which supported the existence of the army that made Bismarck's success possible. This, even more than Bismarck's contribution, was the critical factor in bringing about a united Germany.

SECTION 3

Working with Sources

The Special Topic which you study forms the source-based part of the examination, intended to test your ability to work with historical sources of various kinds.

What You are Given

This section of the examination contains a number of source extracts, which may include **primary** and **secondary** sources. You are also told where each source came from: its provenance. This may include the name of the author, a description of the type of source, the title of the source (if it has one) and the date of its creation or publication. This is intended to help you to decide if it is a primary or secondary source and if the author was involved personally in the events or issue to which the source refers.

PRIMARY AND SECONDARY SOURCES

A primary source is either one which was written or created at the time of the events concerned, or one which was written later by someone who was alive at the time, reflecting on their own memories of the period. Among the contemporary sources there may be speeches, letters, newspaper articles, cartoons, posters, pictures or books. Later works which can still be regarded as primary because they represent first-hand knowledge are likely to be books, often memoirs, published in later years. When you see that a book was published 20, 30 or more years after the events which it discusses, do not assume that this makes it a secondary source. If it describes and comments on personal experiences, it should be regarded as a primary source.

Secondary sources are ones which are not based on personal involvement at the time, but which interpret historical events from a study of the surviving evidence. Typically, these are taken from articles or books written by historians who have studied the period concerned.

Differences Between Primary and Secondary Sources

The historian Eric Hobsbawm once wrote, 'What the contemporary observer sees is not necessarily the truth, but the historian ignores it at his peril.' *Industry and Empire* (1968). This explains why you are asked to evaluate contemporary sources. Just as historians interpret historical evidence in different ways, so people who participate in the events have different ways of seeing the events in which they were involved.

If you doubt this, think of a simple event like a traffic accident. Apart from the drivers, whose opinions are likely to be coloured by personal involvement, there may be half a dozen witnesses whose views of the accident will vary depending on how far they were from the collision, which way they were facing, how good their eyesight is, how much attention they were paying and a host of other factors. The police officer investigating has to take statements from them all, doubtless containing some conflicting evidence, and reach a balanced conclusion on what actually happened and who, if anyone, was to blame.

Witnesses to historic events are subject to even more influences than those of witnesses to an accident. Even those who are involved almost certainly do not know the whole story. In any case, their accounts are likely to be biased by their own prejudices and by the natural desire to appear in a good light themselves. Those whose involvement is less direct have to base their opinions on what they learn from public statements or through the media. To give an instance from events in 1995, interpretations of the war in the former Yugoslavia will be vastly different when given by people whose knowledge of the war comes in different ways. A future historian may be faced by many versions of the events from, say:

- Slobodan Milosevic, the President of Serbia;
- Mohamed Sacirbey, the Foreign Minister of Bosnia;
- Franjo Tudjman, the President of Croatia;
- individual Bosnian, Croatian and Serb refugees who have lost homes and families due to the fighting;
- a Bosnian Serb soldier who is afraid of being accused of war crimes;
- soldiers who have served with the UN peacekeeping forces;
- western journalists who have visited the war zone;
- people in Britain who have read about the war in the newspapers and watched television reports of the fighting.

It would hardly be realistic to expect all of these people to agree. The task of the historian is to evaluate their evidence and to try to come as close to the truth as possible. The same is true of any period in History.

It is not correct, then, to form the equation: primary = accurate and reliable. The primary source may tell you as much about the author as it does about the issue to which it relates. Avoid the temptation to assume that a primary source is right and a secondary source about the same topic is wrong, just because the primary source was written nearer the time.

Of course, the fact that a secondary source is written by someone who has studied the period gives it both advantages and disadvantages. One advantage is the fact that the historian does not have the immediate, often emotional, involvement in the events and the passage of time provides the ultimate result of events, giving the historian the benefit of hindsight. The secondary source is also based on a study of a wider range of evidence, allowing the writer to compare the primary accounts and test one piece of evidence against others, which should allow a more accurate interpretation to be made. As with primary sources, this does not lead to the conclusion that secondary = accurate, because the historian may also be biased or may not have access to all the important evidence. The secondary source is a considered to be an interpretation, but as you know (see page 10) interpretations tend to change as fresh evidence is uncovered.

The best advice on evaluating sources (primary and secondary) is to read them in the light of your own understanding of the period being studied. After all, your interpretation is just as valid as mine or anyone else's, as long as you can justify it by careful assessment of the evidence.

'Source-Handling' Questions

The questions in this part of the examination are intended to test your ability to:

'... comprehend, interpret and compare sources, place sources in their historical context, assess the value and reliability of sources, identifying viewpoint and bias and commenting on inaccuracies and gaps in evidence.'
Revised Arrangements in History, Scottish Examination Board (1990)

This range of purposes can only be achieved by setting a variety of types of question, each concentrating on one or more of these skills. It is just as essential that you understand the question before you begin to answer this type of exercise, as when you are preparing to write an essay. Once again, you should be asking yourself, 'What does the question ask me to **do**?'

SOURCE COMPREHENSION

These are some examples of the type of question you can expect to be asked in this part of the exam. The simplest kind of question is one which asks you to show your understanding of a single source. Here are some ways in which these could be phrased:

What does Source X reveal about . . .?
According to Source X, why did Britain adopt a policy of appeasement in the 1930s? (Special Topic – Appeasement and the Road to War)
Why did Britain and France adopt a policy of non-intervention in the Spanish Civil War? Refer to Source X in your answer. (Special Topic – Appeasement and the Road to War)
In what ways does Source X justify United States intervention in Vietnam in the 1960s? (Special Topic – the Cold War)

In questions of this sort, you are being asked to explain the point being expressed in the source. This does not mean simply copying out the detailed information given in the source, but identifying the main argument and using the detail to explain this argument.

Here is a source dealing with British reaction to Hitler's reoccupation of the Rhineland in March 1936. It is taken from a speech in the House of Commons by the Labour MP Hugh Dalton, on 20 March 1936.

> It is only right to say bluntly and frankly that public opinion in this country would not support, and certainly the Labour Party would not support, the taking of military sanctions or even economic sanctions against Germany at this time … Public opinion here does, I think, draw a clear distinction between the action of Signor Mussolini in resorting to aggressive war and the actions, up-to-date at any rate, of Herr Hitler which … have taken place within the frontiers of the German Reich.

A question based on this source could read,

> *What does the source reveal about opinion in Britain about action against Germany following the reoccupation of the Rhineland?*

Because it only asks you to show your understanding of the source, a question like this is likely to be worth only 4 marks. To gain these, you must:

- identify the author's argument;
- show your understanding of the case he or she is arguing;
- comment on what this reveals about the issue.

It may also be relevant to say something about the author and his or her background.
In this case, the information that should be included in your answer is:

- Hugh Dalton and his party are opposed to Britain taking any action, military or economic, against Germany at this time;
- he believes that the British public is against any such action;
- the reason for this attitude is that, unlike Mussolini with his invasion of Abyssinia, Hitler has acted only with the frontiers of his own country.

You could also comment that the source only reveals one of the arguments against intervention and that it does not discuss opposing views.

Read this source, which is taken from a speech in the House of Commons by the Prime Minister, Neville Chamberlain, on 8 April 1938, then make a list of the points that you could make in answering the question which follows:

Our policy is not one of dividing Europe into two opposing *blocs* of countries, each arming against the other amidst a growing flood of ill-will on both sides, which can only end in war. That seems to us to be a policy which is dangerous and stupid. You may say we may not approve of dictatorships ... We cannot re-move them. We have to live with them ... We should take any and every op-portunity to try to remove any genuine and legitimate grievance that may exist.

In what ways does the source explain the British Government's policy of appeasement?

You can compare your list with the one on page 66.

COMPARING SOURCES

You are likely to meet four kinds of source-comparison question. In the first, you are asked to compare two sources, often ones expressing conflicting views. Sometimes you may be asked just to identify the differences between the sources. Questions which do this might read like this:

> *Compare the views expressed in Sources X and Y on Irish involvement in World War I. (Special Topic – Ireland 1900–85).*
> *In what ways do Sources X and Y differ about the* Anschluss *of 1938? (Special Topic – Appeasement and the Road to War).*

In order to answer questions like these, the first stage is the same as in compre-hension questions. Before you can compare the views outlined in two (or more) sources you must identify what the sources actually say. To take the first example above, Source X, written by a Unionist politician, might argue that Irishmen, as citizens of the British Empire, have a duty to volunteer for service in the forces. The other, perhaps written by a nationalist, might maintain that Britain's quarrel is not Ireland's quarrel, so they should have nothing to do with it. Your answer should begin by showing clearly that you understand the major difference be-tween the sources, that Source X favours Irish participation in the war, while Source Y opposes it. Once you have done this, you should explain each of the views in more detail, summarising each author's reasons in support of their indi-vidual argument. In doing this, there can be a great temptation to copy out chunks of the source. Try to resist this temptation, as it does not demonstrate your historical understanding, only your mechanical ability to copy words from one sheet of paper onto another. You will gain higher marks by using your own words.

It will also help to convince the examiner that you understand the sources and the issue if you refer to their authorship. This need not be a lengthy analysis, and should certainly not follow practices you may have used at Standard Grade by saying that a source is primary because it was written at the time, that it was writ-ten as a piece of propaganda so may not be reliable and so on. A passing com-ment will often make the point very well:

'The author of Source Y uses an argument, typical of views among national-ists in 1914, that ...'

The point is made but is not laboured and you have saved time that can be used more usefully elsewhere.

This approach, useful though not required in straight comparison questions, is essential for the second style of question, which asks you to go a step further, and explain the disagreement between the sources. Examples of this kind of question could be:

> *Explain why Sources X and Y differ about the results of Irish immigration on the lives of Scottish people in the mid-nineteenth century. (Special Topic – Patterns of Migration.)*

Here is a question referring to two sources on the Czech crisis of 1938:

Source A: from a press release by Winston Churchill MP, 21 September 1938.

> The partition of Czechoslovakia under pressure from England and France amounts to the complete surrender of the Western Democracies to the Nazi threat of force. Such a collapse will bring peace or security neither to England nor to France. On the contrary, it will place these two nations in an ever weaker and more dangerous situation. The mere neutralisation of Czechoslovakia means the liberation of twenty-five German divisions, which will threaten the Western front ... It is not Czechoslovakia alone which is menaced, but also the freedom and the democracy of all nations.

Source B: from the leading article, The Times, *1 October 1938.*

> No conqueror returning from a victory on the battlefield has come home with nobler laurels than Mr Chamberlain from Munich yesterday ... He has not only relegated an agonizing episode to the past; he has found for the nations a new hope for the future. The joint declaration made by Herr Hitler and Mr Chamberlain ... shall govern the whole of their relationships.

> *What differences of opinion about the Czech crisis of 1938 are revealed by comparing Sources A and B?*

The first thing to do is to work out what the main disagreement is between the sources. This, of course, is that Churchill opposes giving way to German demands over Czechoslovakia, while *The Times* praises the Prime Minister for signing the Munich Agreement, which gave Hitler the Sudetenland.

Looking into the sources in more detail, it becomes clear that the difference of opinion runs deeper than this. *The Times* is optimistic that, by resolving the Czech problem and signing the joint declaration, Hitler and Chamberlain have made possible a new and more peaceful atmosphere between Britain and Germany, which can bring hope to all countries. In contrast, Churchill warns that the break up of Czechoslovakia only increases the danger to other countries, especially the Western allies, by releasing German troops to face them in the west.

You could add to this discussion by referring to Churchill's well-known opposition to the policy of appeasement and the fact that *The Times* generally supported the government, so both sources represented well-established points of view. Note that, although it is not of great significance for this question, the press release from Churchill is dated just before the second of Chamberlain's three visits to Germany, so is not commenting on the Munich Agreement itself but warning in advance against dividing up Czechoslovakia, while *The Times* is welcoming Chamberlain home after the signing of the Agreement. For some questions, this difference could be very important, so you should take note of the exact dates of contemporary sources, in case they have an effect on your evaluation of the sources.

Look at a question from the 1994 examination, based on these two sources:

Source C: from J Gurney, Crusade in Spain *(1974).*

> The Spanish Civil War seemed to provide the chance for a single individual to take a positive and effective stand on an issue which seemed to be absolutely clear. Either you were opposed to the growth of Fascism and went out to fight against it, or you acquiesced in its crimes and were guilty of permitting its growth. There were many people who claimed it was a foreign quarrel and that nobody other than the Spaniards should involve themselves in it. But for myself and many others like me, it was a war of principle, and principles do not have national boundaries. By fighting against Fascism in Spain, we would be fighting against it in our own country, and every other.

Source D: from a speech made by Anthony Eden MP, the Foreign Secretary, 12 April 1937.

> The policy of non-intervention has limited and bit-by-bit reduced the flow of foreign intervention in arms and men into Spain. Even more important, the existence of that policy, the knowledge that many governments, despite all discouragement, were working for it, has greatly reduced the risk of a general war...
> Six months ago, I told the House of Commons of my conviction that intervention in Spain was both bad humanity and bad politics. Nothing that has happened since has caused me to modify that judgement; some events have caused me to confirm it.

In what ways, and for what reasons, do Sources C and D differ over the policy of non-intervention in the Spanish Civil War? (6 marks)

In preparing your answer, remember to consider both parts of the question. Start by identifying the overall disagreement between the sources, then explain the detailed points on which they disagree. Finally, consider the authorship of the sources and see if that helps to explain their viewpoints. In this kind of question, it is as important as in an essay to come to a proper conclusion, so write a single sentence summing up the main differences between the sources. Now compare your answer with my ideas on pages 66–67.

Comparing Several Sources

The third form of source comparison question which is fairly common is one which asks you to compare several sources. Typically, this question asks you to say either how far some primary sources support an historian's view of a particular issue or how fully the named sources explain an issue. As these questions are more demanding, they usually carry seven or eight marks.

The process of answering questions which ask you to compare several sources is very like that involved in comparing two sources: identifying the main point being made in each source and its supporting evidence, and then looking for points of agreement or disagreement between them. With a group of sources, though, your answer will be longer, and it may be helpful to treat it as a short essay.

Here are two examples of how this might work. In the first, you are asked to consider how well three primary sources support the opinions of an historian:

Source A: from Martin Gilbert, Britain and Germany between the Wars *(1964).*

> Chamberlain did not see why Germany should be Britain's enemy. He realised that, as a result of her defeat in 1918 and of the terms laid down at Versailles, her grievances were not those of ambition ... alone: she sought equality – of status and of advancement.
>
> For Chamberlain appeasement was a comprehensive policy of giving Germany her rightful place in Europe, and by doing so, to make her a contented and gentler member of the European community. Those that sought to 'appease' Germany did so, not necessarily because they feared German ambitions, but because they recognised those ambitions as just, and feared lest, by thwarting them they might drive Germany to violence.

Source B: from a speech by the Conservative leader, Stanley Baldwin, in the House of Commons, November 1932.

> I think it is well also for the man in the street to realise that there is no power on earth that can protect him from being bombed. Whatever people may tell him, the bomber will always get through. The only defence is offence, which means that you have to kill more women and children more quickly than the enemy if you want to save yourselves.

Source C: from a speech by Neville Chamberlain in the House of Commons, 26 July 1938.

> If only we could find some peaceful solution of this Czechoslovakian question, I should myself feel that the way was open again for a further effort for a general appeasement – an appeasement which cannot be obtained unless we can be satisfied that no major cause of difference or dispute remains unsettled ... [The Anglo-German Naval Treaty] stands as a demonstration that it is possible for Germany and ourselves to agree upon matters which are vital to us both.

Source D: from a letter written by a Foreign Office official, Sir Orme Sargent, 30 December 1946, reflecting on the pre-war years.

> [Appeasement] stands condemned solely because it was ineffective, because it was bound to be ineffective and because Chamberlain ought to have known it would be ineffective. He had only to study Hitler's technique – and he ought to have been studying it ever since 1933 – in order to realise that Hitler would be prevented from responding to any sort of appeasement by his own temperament ... and by all that he stood for in the eyes of the great and fanatical party which he had created and which was governing Germany.

How far do Sources B, C and D support Gilbert's analysis of the policy of appeasement in Source A? (8 marks)

To introduce this answer it is necessary to say what Martin Gilbert's analysis of the policy of appeasement actually is. He says that those who supported the policy did so because they believed that Germany had a good case for a review of the terms of Versailles and that appeasing their grievances would bring a more stable peace to Europe. To do otherwise risked Germany settling its grievances through aggression.

It is now necessary to compare each of the other three with this analysis. Source C, for example, supports Gilbert in that Neville Chamberlain himself gives his own reasons for appeasement during the Czech crisis. He expresses the opinion that if that crisis could be solved in a peaceful way it would allow the negotiation of a solution to all of the outstanding problems in Europe – in his words 'a general appeasement'. Gilbert's point that Chamberlain did not see Britain and Germany as inevitable enemies is also supported by his comments on the success of the Naval Treaty in resolving peacefully a potential area of dispute. Source B, on the other hand, suggests a very different motive for appeasers: fear of the bomber and its impact on the civilian population. You could argue that this disagrees with Gilbert's view of appeasement as a wish to settle just grievances. Source D also casts some doubt on Gilbert's views by its observation that Chamberlain ought to have known better than to consider the possibility of dealing reasonably with Hitler simply by looking at his record and at every message coming out of Germany. While Gilbert appears sympathetic at least to Chamberlain's motives, Sargent is critical of his policy as being unrealistic.

Your answer to questions of this length cannot be allowed to die away without a short conclusion which answers the question. This rounds off your answer and leaves the examiner sure you know what you have been doing. Here, it could read like this:

> Gilbert sees appeasement as a constructive policy aimed at giving peace to Europe by taking away the causes of Germany's aggressive policies. This is supported by Chamberlain's own statement in Source C, but Source B sees it more as a response to the fear of air power in a future war, and Source D claims that such a policy could never have worked, and that this should have been obvious to the appeasers at the time.

Using some of the same sources, the question could have asked for a different angle on the issue:

> *How fully do Sources A, B, and C explain the policy of appeasement in the 1930s?*

Again, you would identify the main points from the sources, saying that between them these sources showed the appeasers' desire to form a lasting basis for peace by removing the just grievances of Germany over Versailles, their belief in the possibility of the European countries making agreements to resolve differences, as shown in the Naval Treaty, and the influence of the belief that aerial bombardment would be devastating in any future war. In this case, you would then bring in your own recalled knowledge to show that these sources did not explain the policy fully. As evidence of this, you could mention their awareness of public opposition to war, especially as seen in the activities of peace movements, and perhaps also concerns about the state of readiness of the armed forces. Again, a conclusion which briefly draws together your ideas will help you to gain the highest marks.

Choosing Between Views

The final way in which you can be asked to compare sources is to make a judgement about which of two given sources is more accurate, reliable or valuable as evidence about an issue. Here are some examples of how such questions might be phrased:

> *Does Source X or Source Y reflect more accurately opinion at the time about . . .?*
> *From your knowledge of the period, does Source X or Source Y provide more accurate evidence about . . .?*
> *Does Source X or Source Y give the more accurate interpretation/analysis of . . .?*
> *Do you agree with the author of Source X or Source Y about . . .?*

As usual, the starting point for questions of this sort is explaining what the sources actually say and identifying the ways in which they differ, as in a direct source comparison question. On this occasion, though, you must take the process a stage further, by making a judgement between them. The only way you can do this properly is by supporting your opinion by using recalled knowledge.

This can be illustrated by an example from the Special Topic, *Ireland 1900–85: A Divided Identity*. The sources relate to the actions of the British authorities after the Easter Rising of 1916.

Source A: from a letter from General Maxwell, the British army commander, to Prime Minister Asquith, 1916.

> In view of the gravity of the Rebellion and its connections with German intrigue and propaganda, and in view of the great loss of life and destruction of property …, the General Officer Commanding in Chief, Irish Command has found it imperative to inflict the most severe sentences on the organizers of this detestable Rising and on the Commanders who took an actual part in the actual fighting which occurred. It is to be hoped that these examples will be sufficient to act as a deterrent to intriguers and to bring home to them that the murder of His Majesty's subjects or other acts calculated to imperil the safety of the realm will not be tolerated.

Source B: from a letter from George Bernard Shaw to the Daily News, *10 May 1916.*

> My own view … is that the men who were shot in cold blood after their capture or surrender were prisoners of war, and that it was, therefore, entirely incorrect to slaughter them …
> Until Dublin Castle is superseded by a National Parliament … an Irishman resorting to arms to achieve the independence of his country is doing only what Englishmen will do if it be their misfortune to be invaded and conquered by the Germans in the course of the present war … It is absolutely impossible to slaughter a man in this position without making him a martyr and a hero.

> *Does Source A or Source B give a more accurate analysis of the results of British actions after the Easter Rising of 1916?*

The first step in answering this question is to say that Source A tries to justify the punishment of the leaders of the Rising and claims it would prevent others from rebelling in future, and that Source B condemns the punishments, saying that they were unjustified and would simply turn the victims into martyrs, inspiring others to take their places. In this case it would be well worth commenting on the bias of Source A, which was written by the officer who ordered the punishments.

Having identified these points, from your learning you could include the information that the Easter Rising of 1916 was in fact not a great threat to the government either in London or in Dublin. Its support was so small that there was no chance of its succeeding in setting up the Irish Republic which the rebels proclaimed. This suggests that Source A exaggerated the peril to the state and to the King's subjects. The contrast could be made between the General's view of the men as 'intriguers' and rebels, and Shaw's description of them as 'prisoners of war' and fighters for independence. You could mention that Shaw's prediction came all too true, as the executed leaders were indeed regarded as martyrs, their deaths convincing many Irish people who had not been strong nationalist supporters to support them in future. In conclusion, you could bring in your knowledge that, within two years, Irish nationalist organisations were able to fight the British more strongly, making Shaw's analysis more convincing than that of General Maxwell.

3 Read these sources which describe differing views on the *Anschluss* of 12 March 1938, then answer the question after them, using recalled knowledge as well as the sources in your answer. Questions of this type usually carry five or sometimes six marks, so your answer should contain about five clear points and end with a sentence which answers the question directly.

Source A: from a letter from Thomas Moore, a Conservative Member of Parliament, to The Times, *17 March 1938.*

> If the Austrian people had not welcomed this union, physical opposition and bloodshed must have occurred. That so far there has been none proves the inherent desire of the two nations to secure the *Anschluss* of which they have been so long deprived by the determined interference of the leading European powers … [Austria] has free markets for her raw materials and manufactured goods, but, more important still, she is removed as a source of friction and discord from international relationships.

Source B: from a speech by Winston Churchill in the House of Commons, 14 March 1938.

> The gravity of the event of March 12 cannot be exaggerated. Europe is confronted with a programme of aggression, nicely calculated and timed, unfolding stage by stage, and there is only one choice open, … either to submit like Austria, or else to take effective measures while time remains to ward off the danger and if it cannot be warded off to cope with it … If we go on waiting upon events, how much shall we throw away of resources now available for our security and the maintenance of peace? How many friends will be alienated, how many potential allies shall we see go one by one down the grisly gulf?

Does Source A or Source B reflect more accurately British opinion at the time about the Anschluss *of March 1938?*

My ideas about what the answer should contain are on page 67.

RELATING A SOURCE TO YOUR KNOWLEDGE OF THE PERIOD

The syllabus for Revised Higher Grade History says that one of the skills you are expected to demonstrate is the ability to 'place sources in their historical context'.

This is much easier than it sounds, as long as you recognise that is what the question is asking you to do. In fact, you are being asked to use your recalled knowledge to demonstrate some of the skills mentioned at the beginning of this section (pages 43–45): assessing value and reliability, identifying bias, commenting on accuracy and gaps in evidence. In the last questions on comparing sources you have been showing these skills already by using your recalled knowledge to make judgements about them. Sometimes, you are asked to place a single source in context. The question will give you a clue that this is necessary.

Here are some examples of questions that ask you to relate your knowledge to the sources in slightly different ways:

ASSESSING VALUE AND RELIABILITY

Sometimes, this kind of question will be based on a pictorial source, such as a cartoon. Although some people worry about the difficulty of picking out evidence from a source which is intended to be humorous, this very fact often makes the cartoon an easy source to use, as the cartoonist has to make the point very clearly for people to find it funny. Page 56 shows an example, from the 1992 examination, which uses a very famous cartoon that is loaded with possible points. The question about the source is:

Explain the significance of Source A in the context of events at the time.

There are three stages in answering a question like this.

- Identify the main points made in the source.
- Select relevant information from your recalled knowledge that will help you to comment on the points made in the source.
- Compare what you know with what the author has said and draw a conclusion which refers back to the question.

EVIDENCE FROM THE SOURCE

In this case, there is a wealth of information in the source.

- Germany is shown as a heavily armed goose, though it has a laurel branch, the sign of peace, in its mouth along with the label *Pax Germanica* which means 'German peace'.
- The windows of the houses are filled with swastika flags, suggesting that the people of the area welcomed the German reoccupation.
- The goose is shown trampling on the torn up Treaty of Locarno.
- The cartoon, in showing Germany as militaristic and aggressive, did not reflect the common view that her action was justified, but was much closer to the minority view of Churchill and his colleagues who wanted to oppose Hitler as early as possible.
- The cartoon was drawn in the same month as the reoccupation took place.

THE GOOSE-STEP.

"GOOSEY GOOSEY GANDER,
WHITHER DOST THOU WANDER?"
"ONLY THROUGH THE RHINELAND—
PRAY EXCUSE MY BLUNDER!"

Source A: a cartoon by Ernest H Shepard in Punch, *March 1936.*

- The goose itself is a visual joke because the German army used the goose step as its marching step.
- The use of the word 'Only' in the caption suggests the action is not a very serious one.

EVIDENCE FROM RECALL

- Germany did reoccupy the Rhineland using military force in March 1936.
- This action did destroy the agreement made at Locarno in 1926 as well as breaking the terms of the Treaty of Versailles.
- Most people in the Rhineland welcomed their reunion with Germany.
- Britain and France did nothing to oppose Germany's actions.
- Some people in Britain were alarmed by the reoccupation, but many others took the view that Germany was only reclaiming territory which was rightfully hers, and regarded it as resolving a problem created at Versailles.

COMMENT ON SIGNIFICANCE

- The cartoon is very useful because comparing its picture of German actions with what really happened shows that the cartoonist's knowledge of what was happening was accurate.

It may look as though there is a great deal to do here, especially as the question was worth only four marks. Of course, I have included practically everything that could be said here, but it would not be necessary to pick out all of these points in order to score well. What is important is that you pick out some of the important points made by the cartoonist – the first four I have given you above are the most important – and that you compare these with your knowledge enabling you to comment on how useful or accurate the source is. It is not necessary or even desirable to do this in the order I have given here, which would seem artificial in a real answer. It was only done to show the three steps separately. In your answer you should compare the points in the source with those from your knowledge in the way which seems most natural, which in most cases means taking one piece of information from the source at a time and connecting it with your knowledge.

Here is a similar question from the 1991 examination, putting a cartoon in context, taken from the Special Topic, *The Origins and Development of the Cold War.*

Source A: a Punch *cartoon, October 1956.*

Explain the significance of the cartoon (Source A) in the light of events at the time. (5 marks)

Your tasks remain as before. You must identify the main points made in the cartoon and use your recalled knowledge to place the cartoon in context and reach a conclusion. Once more, the cartoon is so good that you are spoiled for choice in choosing evidence from it.

EVIDENCE FROM THE SOURCE

- Khrushchev is portrayed as a bear tamer, representing Soviet attempts to keep their satellites (the bears) in their places.
- Bulgaria, Albania and Czechoslovakia are obedient, but the bear which represents Yugoslavia has left its block and is ignoring the trainer completely, even looking for a way out of the cage, while Hungary and Poland are leaving their blocks.
- If you are very observant, you may notice that the expressions on the faces of the bears give clues about their attitudes towards the trainer. Some of these are very funny indeed.

EVIDENCE FROM RECALL

- The cartoon was drawn in October 1956, a few weeks before the repression of the Hungarian Revolt.
- By then, Tito's Yugoslavia was pursuing a very independent line and Poland, like Hungary, was showing signs of discontent.
- Khrushchev, as Soviet leader, was faced with the prospect of the Eastern *bloc* breaking up altogether if action was not taken to re-establish control.

The process in dealing with a written source is just the same. In this example from the Special Topic, *The Origins and Development of the Cold War*, a similar question could be asked about this source:

Source X: from a speech by President John F Kennedy in West Berlin, 26 June 1963.

> Today, in the world of freedom, the proudest boast is *Ich bin ein Berliner* [I am a Berliner].
>
> There are many people in the world who do not understand what is the great issue between the free world and Communists. Let them come to Berlin. And there are some who say in Europe and elsewhere that we can work with the Communists. Let them come to Berlin.
>
> Freedom has many difficulties and democracy is not perfect; but we never had to put up a wall to keep our people in. I know of no city which has been besieged for 18 years and still lives with the vitality, force, hope and determination of this city of West Berlin ...
>
> In 18 years of peace and good faith this generation of Germans has earned the right to be free, including the right to unite their family and nation in lasting peace with the goodwill of all people.

Comment on the significance of Source X in the light of events at the time.

In this source, President Kennedy made clear that he believed there were real differences between the Western powers and the Soviet *bloc* and that the Western way of life was superior to that of the Communist countries. He pointed to the building of the Berlin Wall as evidence of that superiority, as such action had never been needed to prevent people leaving the West. He also praised the people of West Berlin for standing up to the pressures from the East, and stated his opinion that Germany ought to be allowed to reunite.

From recalled knowledge it could be pointed out that this source is not only valuable as a statement of United States policy but as a very significant occasion in itself. This was one of the most famous speeches ever made by President Kennedy, whose purpose was to encourage the people of West Berlin and West Germany at a time when there was great fear of a potential Warsaw Pact attack on West Germany and to warn the Soviet Union not to be tempted into any aggressive act. The President's support for reunification of Germany was also significant, for at the time the main opponents of such unification were the Soviet Union and its allies.

Note that questions of this sort can be phrased in other ways, without affecting greatly what you have to do. For example, the question above would have had a very similar meaning if it had read:

> *How valuable is Source A as evidence about the Berlin crisis?*
> or *How useful is Source A as evidence about the policy of the United States towards Berlin in 1963?*

With another source, the question may ask you directly:

> *How reliable is Source X as evidence about (a named issue).*

This is again a question with the same intention, to ask you to make a judgement about the source as evidence.

Here are four sources, taken from different Special Topics. Read the source which refers to the Special Topic which you are studying, then make lists of the points you could take from the source and from recall in order to answer the question.

> *Comment on the historical significance of the Source in the light of events at the time.*

Special Topic: *Patterns of Migration: Scotland 1830s–1930s*
From the Ayr Advertiser, *1849.*

Over the greater part of Scotland a deplorable change is at the present moment being effected in the habits of the people – a change which is every day becoming more apparent, and forms an increasing cause of alarm to those who have the interest of their native land at heart. Incited by the wretchedness existing in their own country to emigrate to Scotland ... the Irish, during the past ten years, have absolutely inundated this country. They have swallowed up our rapidly increasing poor's rates ... and have filled our jails and penitentiaries; by their great numbers they have either lessened the remuneration, or totally deprived thousands of the working people of Scotland of that employment which legitimately belonged to them ... Let us redouble our efforts not to keep Scotland for the Scotch, for that is impossible; but to keep Scotland – Scotch, Scotch in religion, morality and intelligence.

Special Topic: *Appeasement and the Road to War, to 1939*
From the leading article, Kilmarnock Standard, *5 October 1938.*

The Prime Minister by the Munich agreement has achieved a great success for pacific diplomacy as against threats of violence. It is true that there has been a considerable amount of criticism ... but on the whole the weight of sober opinion remains largely in Mr Chamberlain's favour. The Sudeten Germans ... have never been able to reconcile themselves to Czech rule ... and therefore it must be admitted that there was a racial grievance to be remedied. The Prime Minister has been able to secure a lasting settlement of this controversy without bloodshed. Whatever we may think of Herr Hitler's methods ... the fact remains that the Sudeten Germans ... wanted union with Germany. And that being so, the only practical course to take was that which Mr Chamberlain adopted.

Special Topic: *The Origins and Development of the Cold War 1945–85*
From a speech by President Lyndon Johnson, 7 April 1965.

Over this war – and all Asia – is the deepening shadow of Communist China ... a régime which has destroyed freedom in Tibet, attacked India, and been condemned by the United Nations for aggression in Korea ... The contest in Vietnam is part of a wider pattern of oppressive purposes ... Since 1954 every American President has offered support of the people of Vietnam ... We must say in South-East Asia – as we did in Europe – 'Hitherto shalt thou come but no further'.

Special Topic: *Ireland 1900–85: A Divided Identity*
From a speech by John Redmond in the House of Commons, 15 September 1914.

> For the first time – certainly for over one hundred years – Ireland in this War feels her interests are precisely the same as yours ... She knows that this is a just war. She knows, she is moved in a very special way by the fact that this war is undertaken in the defence of small nations and oppressed peoples ...
> I say that the manhood of Ireland will spring to your aid in this war ... it is their duty, and should be their honour, to take their place in the firing line in this contest.

You can compare your ideas with mine on pages 67–69.

COMMENTING ON ACCURACY AND GAPS IN EVIDENCE

In this form of source evaluation the questions often ask you how far you agree or disagree with the view expressed by the author of the source. As usual, there may be several ways of asking you this:

> *To what extent do you accept the analysis in Source X of ...?*
> *How fully does Source X explain ...?*
> *Do you agree with Source X's explanation of ...?*
> *What justification was there for the views expressed in Source X about ...?*
> *How accurate an assessment does Source X give of ...?*

Although you may be asked to assess a primary source in this way, this kind of question can refer as easily to a secondary source, asking you to evaluate an historian's interpretation of an issue rather than a contemporary observer's view. You should not assume that you must agree with the historian just because he or she is a professional and has probably studied the topic in more depth than you have. The historian's opinions may be based on deeper study than yours, but so are the opinions of all the other historians who have reached different conclusions by interpreting the evidence in different ways. At the risk of becoming repetitive, what matters is not whether you agree with the historian but whether you can argue your case sensibly by reference to appropriate evidence.

Consider this question, based on an extract from *Contemporary Europe: A History* by H Stuart Hughes, published in 1961.

> The Second World War was the work of one man, Adolf Hitler. Of Europe's national leaders, Hitler alone wanted the conflict and brought it about at a moment of his own choosing ...
> The war was the climax of five years of blundering and bluff, of the irresolute diplomacy of the Western powers pitted against the demonic force and unswerving dedication to his goal. Its main origins lay in the successive stages of Nazi expansion.

To what extent do you accept Hughes' analysis of the causes of the Second World War in this source? (6 marks)

The analysis in the source can be summed up quite briefly. Hughes makes two main points.

- Hitler was responsible personally for both for the outbreak of war and even for its timing in 1939.
- The mistakes and weaknesses of the Western powers (Britain and France) helped Hitler to achieve his aims.

One way of answering this question is to show that you recognise this as the traditional explanation of the causes of the war, which was challenged (in the same year as this book was published) by AJP Taylor. Taylor argued that Hitler did not plan the war, but that he had a series of aims in foreign policy for which he was willing to risk war. In 1939 Hitler thought that Britain and France would give way, or at least compromise, over Poland as they had done over Austria and Czechoslovakia. The war broke out because for once he miscalculated. Having shown your awareness of the two sides in the debate, you should say whether or not you agree with Hughes, giving reasons for your decision.

An alternative way to answer this question is by using your recalled knowledge of the period instead of dealing with the historical debate. Among the evidence you might use to evaluate Hughes' argument could be:

- Did Hitler plan the war? Evidence here could include reference to his policy of *Lebensraum* (Living Space) described in *Mein Kampf,* to his determination to overthrow the Versailles settlement or to the summary of an address to his generals in the (admittedly controversial) Hossbach Memorandum.
- Did the weakness of Western leaders contribute to the outbreak of war? Evidence here could include an outline of the policies of collective security and appeasement as well as examples of how the leaders reacted to various events, from the Italian invasion of Abyssinia to the Munich crisis.

With either of these approaches you could find that you have much more information than you need for six marks. As with all of the questions in this section of the examination, it is important not to spend too much time on one question. As a general rule, try to make one properly developed point for each mark available.

Similar questions also occur in other Special Topics, as in this example relating to Ireland 1900–85:

Source X: from Nathaniel Harris, The Easter Rising *(1987).*

> Although it involved the suspension of the Home Rule Act, the outbreak of the First World War actually made the majority of Irishmen less politically militant... The war itself brought prosperity since the army absorbed the unemployed, separation money and similar benefits eased the lot of their wives and children, and wartime needs set up a demand for agricultural goods and stimulated industrial development. A fortnight before the Easter Rising, the Director of Military Intelligence in Ireland reported that: 'The mass of the people are sound and loyal as regards the war, and the country is in a very prosperous state.'

How accurate is the assessment in Source X of the impact of the First World War on Ireland? (6 marks)

You should begin preparing an answer to this question in the normal way, by noting the main points made in the source.

- When the war broke out, most Irishmen stopped taking part in militant campaigns.
- The war actually helped the Irish economy in several ways.
- Early in 1916 there seemed little danger of rebellion.

The next stage is to test these points against your knowledge of the period. In this case, most of the information is accurate, though you could add some detail about the divisions within the nationalist movement over their attitude to the war and about the continued plotting of more extreme groups such as the Irish Republican Brotherhood. You might also wish to make a point about the industrial benefits referred to in the source, being confined mainly to Ulster.

Sometimes, especially with a primary source, you may be asked to decide how accurate or complete is the evidence which it contains. Look again at Source A on page 48, the press release by Churchill during the crisis that led up to the Munich conference. A question linked to that source on its own might be:

How accurate was Churchill's analysis of the international situation in September 1938?

To sum up Churchill's analysis, he regards any division of Czechoslovakia as a defeat for Britain and France, which would give Germany greater military strength and threaten other countries. Now you must show what you have learned about these issues in order to evaluate Churchill's view.

- Some might argue that, short of all-out war, Britain and France had little choice. Geography prevented them from sending troops to defend Czechoslovakia in a limited war. Total war would have been difficult to fight in 1938, as the rearmament process had not yet gone far enough to make the armed forces sufficiently strong to take on Germany with any real prospect of success.

- Others would support Churchill's analysis by saying that the next 12 months proved the accuracy of his fears for Czechoslovakia and for others. Evidence for this view could include the German occupation of Prague in March 1939, the annexation of Memel, and the attack on Poland which provoked Britain and France to declare war on Germany.

A similar style of answer would also be suitable if the question were phrased:

To what extent did later events confirm Churchill's analysis of the international situation in September 1938?

5

Source X: from the editorial of the Dundee Courier and Advertiser, *9 March 1936, following the reoccupation of the Rhineland by Germany.*

There can be little doubt that, by his declarations and actions on Saturday, Herr Hitler has opened a new chapter in Europe's modern History. He has torn up two treaties neither of which is, by its own terms, subject to 'unilateral' repudiation …

The plain truth is that the Treaty of Versailles is in tatters, and the responsibility for that is far from being exclusively Germany's. Recriminations over its violation have become worse than a waste of breath. It was an imposed Treaty, valid just as long as the country on which it was imposed remained too weak to resist. That time passed when Germany re-created her army. If her resurgence was to be resisted it should have been then.

To what extent do you accept the assessment of the international situation in March 1936 given in Source X?

If you were faced with this question:

- What points in the source ought you to discuss?
- What recalled knowledge could you use to help you evaluate these points?
- Write one or two sentences which might form your conclusion.

You can compare your ideas with mine which are on pages 69–70.

TO SUM UP

When working with sources:

1 Work out what the question is asking you to do:
   - show that you understand the source(s)
   - evaluate the source(s) for accuracy, reliability or bias
   - place the source(s) in their historical context
   - compare sources.

2   Identify the main points made in the source(s) and any important detail that you may want to discuss.

3   Identify from your own knowledge any points of information that will help you to carry out the task required.

4   Link these points in as natural a way as possible, using them to explain your argument.

5   Especially in questions carrying larger mark allocations, round off your answer with a conclusion referring back to the question.

SOLUTIONS TO TASKS

Please note that these solutions are not examples of answers that might be written in the examination, but lists of the points that such answers could include.

The main points from the source are:

- The government does not want to see Europe being divided into two armed camps, as that would result in war.
- As the British could not remove dictatorships they had to find a way of living with them.
- To achieve this, and to prevent war, their policy was to remove genuine grievances.

It would also be useful to comment on the timing of this statement. Made less than a month after the *Anschluss* between Germany and Austria, the speech came at a time when the government was under pressure to abandon its policy of appeasement and to stand up to Hitler.

The major difference between the sources is that Gurney was in favour of foreign intervention in Spain, Eden was against. Gurney's reasons were that he hated Fascism and believed it had to be opposed wherever it appeared. By intervening in Spain, he was fighting the whole idea of Fascism, in the hope of preventing its triumph, not only in Spain, but in Britain and everywhere else as well.

Eden's support of non-intervention was based on the argument that intervention, especially by the governments of other countries, would draw the whole of Europe into war. He claimed that the policy was being successful in limiting foreign arms reaching Spain.

Considering the authors, it is clear from what he says that Gurney was a member of the International Brigade who actually went to Spain to fight against Franco, so his views are likely to represent those of Socialists and others who joined that force. You should note that, although this book was published in

1974, Gurney's account is a personal one, expressing beliefs he held at the time and describing his own experiences. It is, therefore, a primary source, just as much as the speech by Eden. His speech was made in his position as Foreign Secretary, so represents official government policy.

You may feel strongly about the views revealed in these sources, agreeing with one and disagreeing with the other. This question is not the place to discuss these. In the paper concerned, the next question asked for your opinions about Eden's assessment of the policy of non-intervention. If you had discussed that in the first question you would have wasted time and been forced to repeat part of your answer in the next one.

(3) Source A is favourable to the *Anschluss,* claiming that both Austrian and German people wanted it and that it had prevented war and helped international relations. Source B is against the *Anschluss,* seeing it as part of an aggressive German plan which must be resisted before other countries suffer the same fate as Austria.

In early 1938, although many people in Britain were alarmed by the expansion of Nazi power, public opinion in general regarded the *Anschluss* as inevitable, as many believed it was unfair for the Versailles Treaty to forbid it. Churchill was still in a minority when he argued for tough resistance to Hitler, though that minority was beginning to grow, as was shown with the resignation of Anthony Eden from his position as Foreign Secretary in February 1938.

(4) **Patterns of Migration**
From the Source

- The source is clearly anti-Irish.
- There had been a large influx of Irish migrants to Scotland over the previous ten years.
- The Irish have become a burden on the poor rates.
- The Irish have been lawless.
- The Irish have taken jobs that could have gone to Scots and have forced down wages.
- There is a need to defend Scottish culture against Irish influences.

From Recall

- Many Scottish newspapers of the time were anti-Irish, and this source reflects that bias.
- The source's claims against the Irish are typical of those put forward by opponents of immigration, especially those regarding lawlessness and their impact on the employment prospects of Scots.
- These claims did have some basis in fact, but were generally much exaggerated. When Irish immigrants got into trouble, it was usually as a result of drunkenness rather than villainy, and the jobs which they were

alleged to have stolen from Scots were usually low-paid, unskilled jobs that were unpopular with the native Scots anyway.

- The last point gives a clue to one possible source of the author's bias in its reference to keeping the 'Scotch religion'. The fact that most of the immigrants were Roman Catholic was a major reason for their finding it difficult to be accepted by the Scots.

Special Topic: Appeasement and the Road to War
From the Source

- Gives approval to Chamberlain's negotiation of the Munich Agreement and praises him for having prevented war.
- Acknowledges that some people have been critical of the Prime Minister, but claims that most people support him.
- Argues that the settlement was the only one possible because the Sudeten Germans wanted to join Germany.

From Recall

- The critics of the Munich settlement like Churchill and Duff Cooper were in a minority, as was shown by the almost hysterical welcome received by the Prime Minister on his return to Britain.
- The source's reference to the settlement as 'lasting' was not an accurate judgement, as Hitler occupied the rest of Czechoslovakia only a few months later, in March 1939.

Special Topic: The Cold War
From the Source

- President Johnson accuses China of being behind the Vietnam conflict as part of a plan to spread Communist rule through Asia.
- He compares the events in Vietnam with those in Tibet and Korea.
- He makes a statement that the United States must prevent this process from going any further.

From Recall

- The argument in the source reflects the 'Domino Theory' that if Vietnam went Communist the other countries of south-east Asia would follow quickly.
- The timing of the speech suggests that it was an attempt to justify the rapid increase in United States involvement in Vietnam at the time.

Special Topic: Ireland

From the Source

- Irish interests in the First World War are the same as Britain's.
- Argument that the war is in defence of small countries and against oppression.
- Irishmen should volunteer to fight in the British army.

From Recall

- John Redmond was the Irish Nationalist leader in the Commons.
- His attitude is explained by his hope that Irish support for the war would encourage Britain to grant Home Rule, the existing Home Rule Bill only being delayed from becoming law by the outbreak of war.
- His attitude was opposed in Ireland by many nationalists, especially republicans, some of whom described Redmond as a traitor.
- Many Irishmen took Redmond's advice and joined the British army.

5

From the Source

- Hitler, by reoccupying the Rhineland, has broken two international treaties. These were not supposed to be broken by any country acting alone.
- It is not only Germany's fault that the Versailles Treaty has been wrecked.
- The Versailles Treaty was forced on Germany, so could only last while Germany was unable to challenge it. Once Germany rebuilt its army, the treaty could not survive.
- The only way the Versailles Treaty could have been protected was by stopping Germany from rebuilding its army.

From Recall

- The two treaties broken by the reoccupation of the Rhineland were Versailles and Locarno.
- Since the 1920s it had been clear that all German governments and the German people resented the Versailles Treaty and wanted it to be scrapped.
- Many people, members of the public and politicians, felt uncomfortable about the treaty and were unwilling to take action to enforce it. This was shown when nothing was done when Hitler walked out of the Disarmament Conference in 1933 or when he announced that Germany was rearming.

Conclusion

The *Courier's* analysis of the situation by 1936 was very accurate. It has been said that the main problem with Versailles was not the Treaty itself but that the Western powers did not have the will to enforce it. This was proved by their re-action to the reoccupation of the Rhineland which showed, once and for all, that the Treaty was dead.

Practice Section

In this section there are questions covering most of the styles of question which can be found in the source-handling section of the examination. They are given for four of the Special Topics, as these represent the ones attempted by almost all candidates who study the Later Modern option.

SPECIAL TOPIC – PATTERNS OF MIGRATION: SCOTLAND 1830s–1930s

Source A: a map of Irish settlement in Scotland, from R Dudley Edwards, An Atlas of Irish History *(1973)*

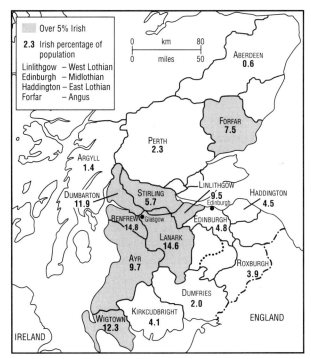

What does Source A reveal about the pattern of Irish settlement in Scotland? (4 marks)

Source B: from the Report on the State of the Irish Poor in Great Britain *(1836).*

The Irish in Edinburgh live chiefly in narrow lanes, in confined, ill-ventilated, damp and dirty situations. In general each family has one room; and in the lodging houses, sometimes there are more than ten or twelve beds in a room. The dwellings of the Irish are not so comfortable or well furnished as those of the Scotch receiving the same wages. Their usual diet is potatoes and occasionally herrings or bacon, they sometimes take porridge – it is rare for them to get meat – they could obtain a better diet if the father, and frequently the mother, were not addicted to the use of spirits.

How accurately does Source B describe the living conditions of Irish immigrants to Scotland in the 1830s? (6 marks)

Source C: from JA Jackson, The Irish in Britain *(1963).*

The rapid growth of cities in Britain … exposed many weaknesses in a public administration which was only able to adapt itself slowly to the changed conditions of urban life. Problems … were aggravated by the rapid rise in population due to migration from rural areas, a general movement in which migration from Ireland represented only a relatively small part. The fact that the Irish areas were singled out for special mention by the numerous commissions concerned to inquire into conditions in the large industrial towns led to the assumption that the Irish were responsible for these conditions … It was perhaps easier for contemporaries to lay the blame at the point that the evil was most evident rather than at its source.

Do you agree with Jackson's assessment of the part played by Irish immigrants in causing poor living conditions in nineteenth-century cities? (7 marks)
To what extent are Jackson's arguments in Source C supported by the evidence in Source B? (6 marks)

Source D: from the Glasgow Evening Post, *23 July 1831.*

On Saturday night the lower part of the city, which had been completely quiet during the whole of the Fair Week, was kept in a state of continued turmoil and disturbance by bands of drunken fellows who poured from the taverns and commenced quarrelling in the streets … The brawls appeared chiefly to be caused by the hordes of low Irish, who … come over to Scotland and bring along with them all their barbarous customs and uncivilised habits, which they practise so frequently, and in such a way, as threatens to ruin the youthful portion of our own intelligent and peaceable population.

How reliable is the evidence in Source D about the behaviour of Irish immigrants in Scotland? (5 marks)

Source E: from the evidence given by Bishop Andrew Scott in the Report of the State of the Irish Poor in Great Britain, *1836.*

A considerable number of ... immoral characters immigrate from Ireland to this country ... The conduct of these people, who from their crimes become best known, is considered by many a part of their national character, and the whole body of the Irish migrants are reproached with their crimes. These reproaches irritate their minds, and tend to keep up a spirit of animosity between them and the natives ... Groundless prejudices against the whole of them exist to a great degree, even among the respectable classes of society. Their naturally warm temper is generally kept in a state of strong agitation, from the continual taunts thrown out by the natives against their country and against their religion, and on ignorant minds this must naturally produce a very bad effect.

Compare the attitudes towards Irish immigrants revealed in Sources D and E. (5 marks)
How fully do Sources B, C, D and E explain the ill feeling between Irish immigrants and native Scots in the mid-nineteenth century? (7 marks)
To what extent had these problems been overcome by the 1930s? (6 marks)

Source F: from evidence given by a mill owner from Blairgowrie, Fourth Report on Intemperance *(1878).*

We have a large Irish Roman Catholic population in Blairgowrie ... They are first-rate workers, and are very well conducted in every way, and the reason is simply this, that the Roman Catholic priest is a man of superior character, a first-rate man. He has for the last twenty years devoted himself night and day to the improvement of his people. He has built a fine school and passed, I think, 98 per cent of his scholars, and even some of the little girls are wonderfully good scholars.

How well does Source F illustrate the importance of the Roman Catholic Church in the lives of Irish immigrants? (6 marks)
How reliable is Source F as evidence of the importance of education to the immigrants? (5 marks)

Special Topic – Appeasement and the Road to War, to 1939

Source A: from a letter to the editor, Glasgow Herald, *28 March 1936.*

What has Germany done? Has she marched into foreign soil, slaughtering semi-defenceless natives as Fascist Italy has? She has simply cast off two of the outworn restrictive articles taken out of the unfair Versailles Treaty and dumped into the Locarno Pact as a 'sop' to French hatred. She has moved some soldiers and equipment, not into foreign territory but merely into another section of the Fatherland soil.

The time has now come for us to recognise that the great German nation has a right to equality with other Powers, and that the disgrace of a dictated treaty cannot be perpetuated. For no fewer than 18 years France has used the League as a means of foisting its whims and bigoted fancies upon other nations of the world.

How reliable is Source A as evidence of attitudes at the time towards the German reoccupation of the Rhineland? (5 marks)

Source B: Pierre-Etienne Flandin, Foreign Minister of France, speaking during a visit to London, c. 12 March 1936, quoted in Winston Churchill, The Gathering Storm.

The whole world and especially the small nations today turn their eyes towards England. If England will act now she will lead Europe. You will have a policy, all the world will follow you, and thus you will prevent war. It is your last chance. If you do not stop Germany now, all is over. France cannot guarantee Czechoslovakia any more, because that will become geographically impossible. If you do not maintain the Treaty of Locarno all that will remain to you is to await a rearmament by Germany, against which France can do nothing. If you do not stop Germany by force today war is inevitable.

What does Source B reveal about the attitude of the French government towards the growing strength of Germany? (4 marks)
In what ways do Sources A and B disagree about the reoccupation of the Rhineland? (5 marks)
To what extent did later events confirm Flandin's analysis in Source B? (6 marks)

Source C: from a memorandum to the Cabinet by Anthony Eden, the Foreign Secretary, January 1937.

The Spanish Civil War has ceased to be an internal Spanish issue and has become an international battleground. The character of the future government of Spain has become less important to the peace of Europe than that the dictators should not be victorious in that country ...
It is therefore my conviction that unless we cry a halt in Spain, we shall have trouble this year ... It follows that to be firm in Spain is to gain time, and to gain time is what we want.

How far do you accept Eden's assessment of the international importance of the Spanish Civil War? (6 marks)

Source D: from JM Roberts, The Age of Upheaval: The World Since 1914 *(1981).*

France and Great Britain had the main burden of standing up to Germany. The Americans were for a long time too much wrapped up in troubles of their own. The Russians were worried by Hitler, but between him and them lay other states, whose help they would need to act against Germany ... This left only France and Britain. They had the unpleasant memory that it had taken four years of bloody fighting and blockade (three of them with Russia on their side) and finally the help of the United States to beat Germany in the Great War. What was more, the two countries were often out of step with one another.

How fully does Roberts in Source D explain the problems facing Britain and France in the 1930s? (6 marks)
To what extent do Sources A, B, C and D reveal the issues concerning the Western powers in the 1930s? (7 marks)

Source E: a cartoon by David Low, 18 July 1938.

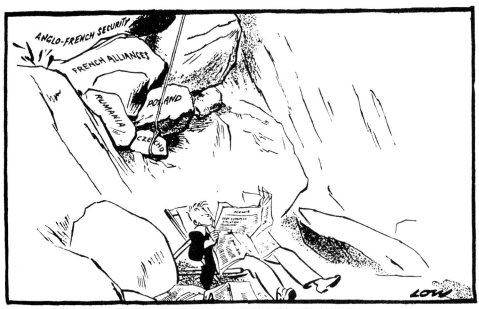

WHAT'S CZECHOSLOVAKIA TO ME, ANYWAY ?

Comment on the significance of the cartoon (Source E) in the light of events at the time. (4 marks)

Source F: adapted from Robert Kee, Munich: the Eleventh Hour *(1988).*

Chamberlain ... acted as he did because, under pressure, he thought it was the right thing to do to let the Germans have the Sudetenland, both as an action in itself and in the interests of the British Empire. It was right, he thought, because the Czechoslovak state had not been particularly well constructed at Versailles. If, by letting the Germans have that territory, there was hope at last of fully appeasing the German spirit which Versailles had made so aggressive, then it was in the interests of the British Empire to do so. Sentiment for Czechoslovakia never troubled him; sentiment for the British Empire, which required international peace and prosperity, did.

To what extent do you accept Kee's analysis of British policy during the Munich crisis of 1938? (6 marks)

SPECIAL TOPIC – THE ORIGINS AND DEVELOPMENT OF THE COLD WAR 1945–85

Source A: from a broadcast on Radio Free Kossuth, 4 November 1956.

Attention! Attention!
Attention! Attention!
Now Imre Nagy, President of the Council of Ministers of the Hungarian People's Republic, is going to address you!
This is Imre Nagy, President of the Council of Ministers of the Hungarian People's Republic. Today at daybreak Soviet forces started an attack against our capital, obviously with the intention to overthrow the legal Hungarian democratic government.
Our troops are fighting.
The government is in its place.
I notify the people of our country and the entire world of this fact.

Comment on the historical significance of Source A in the light of events at the time. (4 marks)

Source B: from an article in Pravda, *23 November 1956, quoted by the United Nations* 'Report of the Special Committee on the Problem of Hungary', *January 1957.*

A Socialist state could not remain an indifferent observer of the bloody reign of Fascist reaction in People's Democratic Hungary. When everything settles down in Hungary, and life becomes normal again, the Hungarian working class, peasantry and intelligentsia will undoubtedly understand our actions better and judge them aright. We regard the help to the Hungarian working class in its struggle against the intrigues of counter-revolution as our international duty.

In what ways, and for what reasons, do Sources A and B disagree about the Soviet invasion of Hungary? (6 marks)

Source C: from an announcement by Nikita Khrushchev, 8 July 1961.

> Comrades, the Government of the Soviet Union is attentively following the military measures taken recently by the United States of America and its NATO allies ...
> The United States' President, Mr Kennedy, has proclaimed in his recent messages to Congress a so-called 'new course'. It provides for stepping up the programme of developing rocket-missile strategic weapons ... A considerable growth of military expenditure is characteristic of Britain, France and other NATO countries ...
> This is how the Western powers are replying to the Soviet Union's unilateral reduction of armed forces and military expenditures carried out over several past years ...
> In view of the growing military budgets in the NATO countries, the Soviet Government has taken a decision to increase defence expenditures in the current year.

How useful is Source C as evidence of the importance of rivalry over military technology in relations between East and West? (6 marks)

Source D: from a televised speech by President JF Kennedy, 22 October 1962.

> The Government, as promised, has maintained the closest surveillance of the Soviet military build-up on the island of Cuba. Within the past week unmistakable evidence has established the fact that a series of offensive missile sites are now in preparation on that imprisoned island. The purpose of these bases can be none other than to provide a nuclear strike capability against the Western Hemisphere.
> This urgent transformation of Cuba into an important strategic base ... constitutes an explicit threat to the peace and security of all the Americas ... This secret, swift and extraordinary build-up of Communist missiles ... is a deliberate, provocative and unjustified change in the 'status quo' which cannot be accepted by this country.

According to Source D, why did the United States regard the Soviet base on Cuba as a threat? (4 marks)

Source E: a message from Nikita Khrushchev to President Kennedy, 27 October 1962, reported in The Times, *29 October 1962.*

> You want to make your country safe. This is understandable; but Cuba too wants the same thing. All countries want to make themselves safe.
> But how are we, the Soviet Union, to assess your actions, which are expressed in the fact that you have surrounded with military bases the Soviet Union, surrounded with military bases our allies; have disposed military bases literally around our country; have stationed your rocket armament there?
> Your rockets are situated in Italy, and are aimed at us. Your rockets are situated in Turkey.
> You are worried by Cuba. You say it worries you because it is a distance of 90 miles by sea from the coast of America.
> But Turkey is next to us. Our sentries walk up and down and look at each other.

How justified was Khrushchev's assessment of the Cuban crisis in Source E? (6 marks)

Source F: from David Horowitz, From Yalta to Vietnam *(1965).*

> By agreeing to withdraw the missiles, Khrushchev lifted the threat of nuclear annihilation from millions whose nations were not involved in the dispute, and hence tended to view the Cuban base as comparable to US bases in Turkey, as well as from those nations who were. And though his action in putting the missiles there in the first place drew harsh criticism, his withdrawal of the missiles in the fact of US intransigence gave him an opportunity to demonstrate moderation ... which he would not otherwise have had ... In retrospect, it would seem that the Soviet Union also gained a 'prestige victory'.
> But Kennedy's triumph, particularly with the Western Alliance and at home, was evident and impressive. From Washington's point of view, the central gain was in dispelling the illusion that the United States would not fight for its vital interests.

To what extent do you agree with the analysis of the outcome of the Cuban crisis by Horowitz in Source F? (6 marks)
How fully do Sources D, E and F explain the issues involved in the Cuban crisis of 1962? (8 marks)

Source G: 'The Train Robbery', a cartoon in Punch, *18 January 1967.*

The Train Robbery

How well does Source G illustrate the effects on the United States of involvement in the Vietnam War? (5 marks)

SPECIAL TOPIC – IRELAND 1900–85: A DIVIDED IDENTITY

Source A: from a speech by John Redmond, MP in the House of Commons, 11 April 1912.

I personally thank God that I have lived to see this day. I believe this Bill will pass into law. I believe it will result in the greater unity and strength of the Empire. I believe it will put an end once and for all to the wretched ill-will, suspicion and disaffection that have existed between this country and Ireland. I believe that it will have the effect of turning Ireland in time … into a happy and prosperous country, with a united, loyal and contented people.

What prevented Redmond's expectations in Source A from coming true? (5 marks)

Source B: from the Solemn League and Covenant, *signed by 471 000 people in Ulster, 28 September 1912.*

Being convinced in our consciences that Home Rule would be disastrous to the material well-being of Ulster as well as of the whole of Ireland, subversive of our civil and religious freedom, destructive of our citizenship, and perilous to the unity of the empire, we, whose names are underwritten, men of Ulster, loyal subjects of His Gracious Majesty King George V, humbly relying on the God whom our fathers in days of stress and trial confidently trusted, do hereby pledge ourselves in solemn covenant throughout this our time of threatened calamity to stand by one another in defending for ourselves and our children our cherished position of equal citizenship in the United Kingdom, and in using all means which may be found necessary to defeat the present conspiracy to set up a Home Rule Parliament in Ireland.

What arguments are used in the Solemn League and Covenant *to justify opposition to Home Rule in Ulster? (4 marks)*
How useful is Source B in explaining the opposition of people in Ulster to the proposal to give Ireland Home Rule? (5 marks)
How justified were the arguments against Home Rule in Source B? (6 marks)
Explain the differing attitudes towards the Home Rule Bill revealed in Sources A and B. (6 marks)

Source C: from a speech by John Dillon MP, in the House of Commons in a debate following the collapse of the Easter Rising in 1916.

I know they were wrong, but they fought a clean fight, and they fought with superb bravery and skill, and no act of savagery has been blamed on any leader or any organized body of insurgents …
As a matter of fact the great bulk of the population were not favourable to the insurrection. The insurgents themselves, who had confidently counted on a rising of the people in their support, were absolutely disappointed. They got no

popular support whatever. What is happening is that thousands of people in Dublin, who ten days ago were bitterly opposed to the whole of the Sinn Féin movement and to the rebellion, are now becoming infuriated against the Government on account of these executions. I am now informed, by letters received this morning, that feeling is spreading throughout the country in a most dangerous degree.

How widely held at the time were the views expressed by Dillon in Source C? (5 marks)

Source D: from CL Mowat, Britain Between the Wars *(1968 edition).*

In 1916, the Volunteers and Sinn Féin came together in the Easter Rebellion in Dublin. Its failure was dismal – until the British government made it glorious by executing in cold blood fourteen of its leaders, and so consecrating with their blood the cause of the Republic they had proclaimed ...
By the summer of 1920 reinforcements for the RIC [Royal Irish Constabulary] were arriving – the notorious Black and Tans ... This is the greatest blot on the record of the Coalition [the British Government led by Lloyd George], and perhaps upon Britain's name in the twentieth century ... For the means used were bound to defeat themselves, and to yield in time to methods of negotiation and compromise.

How well does the evidence in Source C support Mowat's assessment of British actions after the Easter Rising? (5 marks)
From your knowledge of the period, to what extent do you accept the views of Mowat in Source D? (6 marks)

Source E: a cartoon published in Punch, *10 March 1920.*

THE KINDEST CUT OF ALL.

WELSH WIZARD. "I NOW PROCEED TO CUT THIS MAP INTO TWO PARTS AND PLACE THEM IN THE HAT. AFTER A SUITABLE INTERVAL THEY WILL BE FOUND TO HAVE COME TOGETHER OF THEIR OWN ACCORD—(*ASIDE*)–AT LEAST LET'S HOPE SO; I'VE NEVER DONE THIS TRICK BEFORE."

How accurately does Source E illustrate the aims of the Government of Ireland Act of 1920? (6 marks)

Source F: from a speech by Eamon de Valera during a debate in the Dail, December 1921.

My task was to try to get by negotiations something which would satisfy Britain, something which would satisfy what I may call the left wing of the [Irish] Cabinet and something which would satisfy the right wing. The left wing of the Cabinet was for an isolated Republic for the most part but I pulled them over a bit … While I was pulling along that wing, the other wing got away from me.

To what extent does Source F explain the difficulties facing the Irish representatives negotiating the Anglo-Irish Treaty of 1921? (6 marks)

Source G: from the summing up by Judge Theodore Kingsmill Moore in the Sinn Féin funds case, 1948.

Independence and a republic had for so long been considered as essentially the same thing that numbers now found it difficult to conceive of one without the other … Throughout history a flag, a song and a story have counted for more than the arguments of philosophers. With the tricolour, the Soldiers' Song and the shout of 'Up the Republic' the battle had been fought, and now it seemed impossible to accept the first two without the third.

How fully do Sources F and G explain the outbreak of Civil War in Ireland in 1922? (6 marks)

For what reasons did it prove impossible to find a permanent solution to the problem of Irish Home Rule in the period 1912–23? Refer to Sources B, C, D and G in your answer. (8 marks)

3806.